GAME EMBEDDED STRATEGY

Introducing Framework Tn=3
and GEMS for Business Strategy

Patrick A. McNutt

McGraw Hill

Singapore • Boston • Burr Ridge, IL • Dubuque, IA • Madison, WI
New York • San Francisco • St. Louis • Bangkok • Bogotá • Caracas
Kuala Lumpur • Lisbon • London • Madrid • Mexico City • Milan
Montreal • New Delhi • Santiago • Seoul • Sydney • Taipei • Toronto

The **McGraw·Hill** Companies

McGraw Hill Education

Game Embedded Strategy: Introducing Framework Tn=3 and GEMS for Business Strategy

Copyright © 2010 by McGraw-Hill Education (Asia). All rights reserved. No part of this publication may be reproduced or distributed in any form or by any means, or stored in a database or retrieval system, without the prior written permission of the publisher.

4 5 6 7 8 9 10 CTP MPM 20 14 13 12

When ordering this title, use **ISBN 978-007-128892-7** or **MHID 007-128892-9**

Printed in Singapore

Dedication

This book is dedicated to the memory of my parents,
Bill and Ita, and may they rest in peace.

Dedication

Contents

List of Tables	vi
List of Figures	viii
Preface	x
Acknowledgements	xiv
1. Strategic Reasoning	1
2. Game Embedded Strategy	18
3. Baumol Hypothesis	28
4. Marris Hypothesis	38
5. Cost Technology	53
6. Players and Vertical Blending	64
7. Dark Strategy	77
8. Homo Ludens	98
9. Market-as-a-Game	108
10. Market Systems	134
Bibliography	149
Index	153

List of Tables

Table 1.1	Coefficient E: Envy/Entropy	4
Table 1.2	Model Objectives	14
Table 2.1	Typology on Type	22
Table 3.1	Total Revenue Test	32
Table 3.2	Price Elasticity and the Impact of Pricing Decisions Revenue	35
Table 4.1	Return/Risk for *gd*	49
Table 4.2	Marris' Third Variable	50
Table 6.1	Player Types	72
Table 7.1	Game Theory Types	82
Table 7.2	Reply Strategy	83
Table 7.3	Poka-yoke	85
Table 7.4	Blended Management	88
Table 8.1	Prisoners' Dilemma	100
Table 8.2	Volunteer's Dilemma	103
Table 8.3	Classic Prisoners' Dilemma	103
Table 9.1	Homo Ludens	111
Table 9.2	Regret Matrix	119
Table 9.3	Maximin	119

Table 9.4	Regret Criterion	120
Table 9.5	Saddle Point Matrix	122
Table 9.6	Easterbrook–McNutt Strategic Toolbox GEMS	132
Table 9.7	Prisoners' Dilemma	133

List of Figures

| Figure 1.1 | Management Indifference | 12 |

Figure 2.1	Critical Timeline: Nissan	20
Figure 2.2	Nash Premise	21
Figure 2.3	Game Embedded Strategy	25
Figure 2.4	The Wheel of Belief	26

Figure 3.1	Baumol Model	31
Figure 3.2	Trigger Price	33
Figure 3.3	Pricing and Total Revenue Test	36

Figure 4.1	R&D Trade-off	40
Figure 4.2	Marris' Trade-off	43
Figure 4.3	Long-run Operating Equilibrium	45
Figure 4.4	Balanced Growth Path for Apple Inc	50

Figure 5.1	Canon and Cost Leadership Type	54
Figure 5.2	Theoretical Short-run Cost Curve	58
Figure 5.3	Declining LAC	59

Figure 6.1	Market Entry Decision: Extensive Form	69
Figure 6.2	Market Entry Pay-offs: Normal Form	70
Figure 6.3	The Bain-Modigliani Model (Limit Pricing)	76

| Figure 7.1 | Nash Premise | 90 |
| Figure 7.2 | Signal Shower | 91 |

Figure 7.3	Critical Timeline: Apple vs Nokia 2006 – 2008	92
Figure 7.4	Critical Timeline: Apple vs RIM 2007 – 2009	94
Figure 9.1	Bertrand Zero-price Solution	113
Figure 9.2	Bertrand Modified Model	114
Figure 9.3	Critical Timeline: Sony vs Microsoft	115
Figure 9.4	Nash Equilibrium: Sony vs Microsoft	115
Figure 9.5	Dell's Movement in Strategic Focus	127
Figure 9.6	Nomenclature on Type	130
Figure 10.1	ASP and Zero Sum	136
Figure 10.2	Contest Competition	143
Figure 10.3	Hsu-McNutt Signalling	145

Preface

> "Games are nature's
> Most beautiful creation."
>
> ***Leonard Cohen***

The book represents a concise introduction to management type and signalling within the context of business strategy. Type is presented in Chapter 1; this does not refer to personal characteristics or personality type, but rather to the indicator of the consistency and execution of a business strategy. Management are defined as Baumol type (Chapter 3), where the execution of strategy is observed through price signals. The reference is to the classic Baumol model of sales revenue maximisation, wherein pricing enables management to apply their strategy or to meet their objective of maximising sales revenue. Similarly, we refer to Marris type (Chapter 4) and cost leadership type (Chapter 5), where an understanding of type is intricately linked to an economic model. Marris type signals organic growth and cost leadership type signals five steps, notably productivity and capacity.

In the later chapters, we introduce type from a game theory perspective. In this context, the reaction expected from the competitor is influenced by the consistency of a business strategy during a game and the reputation of management as a player keeping to type. In particular, the critical timeline introduced throughout the book looks at the process of modelling observed behaviour, by locating a pattern in the observed data to discover its underlying implication for competitor reaction. Using the critical timeline to capture behaviour allows management an opportunity to estimate the long-term strategic intentions of a competitor by enabling them to take evasive action to avoid losing the game.

Market-as-a-Game

The book also introduces the language and some of the concepts and elements of non-cooperative game theory applied to business decision making. Such an application is not new but the approach we adopt is innovative in its attempt to understand as simply as possible, without diluting its rigorous mathematical reasoning, the game dimension that faces management. In any competition between two players, information is key to winning the game. The market in which the players are competing can be described as a game, and the market-as-a-game acts as a conduit for signals that have the potential to precipitate a reaction from a competitor sooner than the competitor had intended or planned. That, in a nutshell, is this book's *cri de couer*. If management believe signals to be true, the consequent action can no longer be deemed an independent action or decision, and thus management become players in a game.

The real meaning of strategy (Chapters 6 and 7) is found in that dark area of belief and action, where information and truth are vital to the determination of strategy. Captured by a concept called the Nash equilibrium, management as players soon realise that the best outcome in a competitive game is not defined in terms of better profit margins, higher market shares or increased revenues, but rather in terms of the best you can do given the reaction of a competitor, called the near-rival. The discussions in Chapters 8 to 10 describe the game dimension and offer the reader a strategic tool-box to apply in an every-day situation.

The near-rival is introduced to capture the empirical fact that, increasingly, more and more markets are defined as oligopoly, that is, a market structure with five or fewer competing firms. In such a structure, individual management realise that decision making and business strategy is interdependent and not independent of the structure in which they find themselves. What should management do? The theory of oligopoly proposes that management take cognisance of a mutual interdependence in the market, and act accordingly.

The Game Does Not Stop

The game theoretic prescription for the sequential games in oligopoly is that the game stops at a unique Nash equilibrium. However, in the real world of business, strategic thinking is contaminated by learning and experience and players repeat actions in different products and geographies. There is a conflict in the literature between game theory and intuition (Reny, 1993). The market-as-a-game concept in the book (Chapter 9) accepts that when one game stops, a new game begins. In our example of Sony v Microsoft in Chapter 9, the price game ended and a new game on content then began. In March 2009, Microsoft decreased the price on its Xbox models by 30 to 50 per cent, and Sony reacted in the late summer of 2009 ahead of the Tokyo games tradeshow. Both players are observed as repeating their actions and we describe this as learning how to play the market-as-a-game.

The consequences of our decisions at time period t are more likely to accrue in time period $t + 1$ but the time available to make that decision diminishes in time. In other words, the '+1' simply captures the speed at which the reaction occurs so a decision today can lead to a reaction from a competitor in an hour, today, tomorrow or next year. The speed of the reaction is crucial. The competitor most likely to react first and soonest is defined throughout the book as the near-rival. The identification of a near-rival depends on product and geography. Who is the near-rival to Pepsi? One may reply: Coca-Cola. But no, unless one is describing the geography as North America and the product as carbonated soft drinks, more popularly called cola. For example, if the geography is Europe and the product is bottled water, Coca-Cola is unlikely to be Pepsi's near-rival; rather, it could be Nestle or Group Danone.

An Intuitive Rationality

Thinking strategically in the manner just described for Pepsi is at the cusp of Framework $Tn = 3$. The actions and decisions of management are now subject to conflicting motivations and changing belief systems, and, within $Tn = 3$ framework, rational decision making is more about identification of a near-rival than the maximisation of a selfish motive *per se*. Management at Company A may be rational in thinking strategically at time period t not to reduce the price of A's product by x per cent; hence, no price signals are observed from A by its competitors – if management are of the belief that Company B will react, and will react aggressively with a greater price reduction than x per cent. The objective of Framework $Tn=3$ is contained in the hope of understanding business strategy more in line with intuition as observed. The rationality of the management of Company A is intricately linked with their belief about Company B, and this is an intuitive rationality that is co-dependent on the three 'T's' embedded in Framework $Tn=3$: type, technology and time.

Business Strategy

Technology changes the dimension of the game. Observe how the launch of the iPhone has revolutionised the technology of mobile handsets to such an extent that consumers' preferences are time-dependent (the want paradox in Chapter 3) and players evolve. Nokia has evolved to become a content provider. Time has influenced decision making through the kinetic equation $dT/dt = -1$, which limits the time available to make that decision. Often no decision is made but a decision can be signalled in order to allow the player to stay in the game. For example, Nokia is to enter the laptop market. Apple is to offer an iPhone with more business and enterprise functionalities. But it is management type that is an essential part of understanding the intuitive rationality behind business strategy.

It is because of the dynamic interaction between the players and the mutual recognition of their interdependence that management are sequestered as players in the market-as-a-game to gather information from or anticipate gathering information from the observed behaviour of competitors from time period t to $t + 1$. Type is a function of the signals that one observes and the signals provide management with a key insight into the rational behaviour of the competitor (McNutt, 2009). The real meaning of time-varying strategy throughout this book is to be found in the area of belief and action, where an intuitive rational decision to act (or not) is mistake-proofed.

Patrick A. McNutt
November 2009, Dublin and Donegal
www.patrickmcnutt.com

Acknowledgements

> Qui desidarat pacem,
> praeparet bellum
> ***Flavius Vegetius Renatu***

This book expands on the arguments originally presented in the E-book manuscript (McNutt, 2008), which appeared on my webpage, **www.patrickmcnutt.com**. The new book represents an attempt to answer the many queries and critical points raised by colleagues and by the legions of executives who continue to attend my course, Managerial Economics: Economics of Strategy, at the Manchester Business School's MBA programme. This is not a book on game theory per se, nor is it a book on microeconomics. Rather, it is a book that blends the relevant arguments and concepts from each perspective into a new structure called Framework $Tn=3$. The expressed purpose of the framework is to intuitively understand the meaning of business strategy.

The book opens by introducing management type as an example to capture one's experience of signalling in a business context. Type is a function of signals and the signals represent observational learning about the observed behaviour of competitors. I am grateful to the many people and organisations who have provided support and encouragement during the past number of years. Early variants of some of the ideas and concepts have appeared on my webpage and as handouts to executive students on MBA programmes at both University College Galway, and the University of Ulster in Ireland and at Manchester, UK. A 2009 publication in the journal *Homo Oeconomicus* describes a typology for an understanding of type and signals. I am grateful to the editorial board for comments and to all my former students.

I would also like to extend my sincere thanks to the cohorts of students, graduate and undergraduate, who, in the past, at University College Galway and the University of Ulster, and at present at the Manchester Business School, who have listened to and continue to listen to my ideas as they are developed in lectures and seminar. In particular, I wish to acknowledge my appreciation of the very helpful comments and suggestions and case histories received from the present cohort of executives who attend my workshops as part of MBA programme of the Manchester Business School, in particular: Chee Hean, Paul Ballington, Glenn Carney, David Tzu, Giovanni Genna, Say Khoon Lim, Mark Ross, Ann Gill, Amy Chan, Phil Dunglinson, Mohammed Jamoussi, Waseem Haq, Eddy Wong, Sandra Thompson, Lim Cher Chua, Neeraj Gupta, Mark Teo, Maria Valle, Stephen Muncaster, Cristina Alamo, Fransisca Situmorang, Kwame Asare, Pawel Biarda, Robert Claxton, Elbert Loois, Patrick Lim, Kenneth Lai, Clelia Rossi, Elena Demidenko, Joseph Tay, Dan Saunders, Tammi Buckley Jones, Olubunmi Ogundeji, Byran McLoughlin, Yvan Cebenka, Marie-Aimee Tourres, Giovanni Genna, Dandan Zheng, Robert Vass and Alistair Benson. To all of you, may I offer my sincere thanks and appreciation for your comments and suggestions for improvement for the case materials.

My thanks are also extended to the many publishers of the books cited in *Game Embedded Strategy*, for their permission to include their authors' arguments and points of view. In bringing the book to publication, there are a number of people without whose support and assistance the final manuscript would not have been produced. In the construction of some of the diagrams and technical skills that accompany the text, I owe gratitude to Yien Kwok, Phil Boulton and Xavier Duran, as well as to Gerry Long at Standard Printers in Galway for the production of the manuscript. I would also like to thank Jocelyn Lau and Pauline Chua and the production team at McGraw-Hill Education in Singapore for their assistance at every stage of the manuscript, and particularly for their constant encouragement and support. I would like to offer a special thanks to the many scribes and poets whose words of wisdom open each of the chapters.

Interesting books on related themes include the classic and original book by Thomas Schelling, *The Strategy of Conflict* (1960). More modern texts include Roberts (2004): *The Modern Firm: Games, Strategies and Managers* and Nalebuff and Dixit (2008): *The Art of Strategy*. For my MBA students, Baye (2008): *Managerial Economics and Business Strategy* and Besanko (2007): *Economics of Strategy* are recommended. I would recommend these books for a more detailed analysis of the mechanics behind the strategic reasoning in modern game theory.

In the exchange of ideas, I would like to sincerely thank William Baumol, Shanti Chakravarty, Duncan Easterbrook and Manfred Holler for their specific comments on my papers and conference proceedings, and Paul Patton, Paul Taaffe, Xavier Duran, Kevin Jagiello, Bob Ryan, and Charles Schell, for their exchange of ideas along the way. I would like to thank numerous students and MBA executives in class for thoughtful exchanges on how to present the analysis and for the insight shared across the selected case study materials.

I would finally like to thank sincerely my wife, Maeve Doherty, for her constant support and encouragement during the writing of this book.

Patrick A. McNutt

CHAPTER 1

Strategic Reasoning

> "When a lady contemplating a picture in Matisse's studio said to him, 'Surely the arm of this woman is much too long', the artist replied, 'Madame you are mistaken. This is not a woman. This is a picture.'"
>
> ***John Cohen***

Introduction

In the world of business and economics, decisions are made daily. They are reported in the financial press, and commentary on the financial news media channels is instantaneous. Decisions on product launches, the appointment of new chief executive officers (CEOs), and decisions on price, costs and revenues are reported on a daily basis by the financial media. The reports as well as the decisions eventually filter down into a company's performance measures. Guidance from the financial experts is defined in terms of market share movements and profitability numbers. Our premise is that, as more and more decisions are made in the context of time, the time available for making a decision diminishes with time: $dT/dt = -1$. Furthermore, more markets are increasingly characterised by smaller numbers of players whose decisions are wholly interdependent and whose observed behaviour is captured in terms of actions that can lead to a reaction. The actions are signals, and the signals are analysed not just by the financial media but also by competitors in the market. The analysis presented in this book, Framework $Tn = 3$, offers a template with which to comment on the observed signals, a template that focuses on type, technology and time as the three pillars of game embedded strategy.

The theme of the book is management type. This is not a book on game theory per se, nor is it a book on the microeconomics of firm behaviour; it is a book on strategy that draws upon basic arguments in both game theory and microeconomics and distills those arguments into a cohesive setting called Framework $Tn=3$. In defining the economics of strategy, the emphasis will be on management type, technology and time, the three supporting pillars of strategy. Competitors are increasingly in markets where interdependence has become a key parameter in determining market share and profitability. The decline in the market share of Intel can be mirrored by a corresponding increase in the market share of Advanced Micro Devices, Inc (AMD), a condition known as the zero-sum constraint. It becomes a binding constraint when the market share performance of a company reaches an upper bound imposed by the interdependent rivalry with a competitor.

A key feature of a market is that it involves both anonymous and known competitors, opponents with future interaction. Strategy now depends upon the game and the context in which the game is played. The context in which the game is played depends on management and the preferences that guide their behaviour. The behaviour that is observed depends on management type, which is signalled by a variety of real-life situations in the market. For example, if player A reduces prices and player B follows with a matching price reduction, then player B could be described as a follower type. Player A, who initiated the price reduction, may have done so to increase revenues in a certain product range. If so, player A could be described as a Baumol type. So why is type important?

In the example of Intel and AMD, the market can be described by two competing firms, and it is relatively easy for a fact finder to draw an inference on the relative movements in market share. More significantly, both Intel and AMD management are aware of the two companies' interdependence. However, in markets with more than two competing firms it is more difficult to isolate an upper bound, and more difficult to identify the competitor whose market share increase mirrors one's own decrease unless management take cognizance of type, technology and time in their strategy. Notwithstanding shifts in demand in existing markets, new products and innovation in emerging markets, more consumers at the point of sale, and increasing volumes, unless market shares are at best increasing or stable the zero-sum constraint applies. In expanding markets, for example, mobile telephony or Internet search engines, management will experience an upper bound at a point in time, and when it translates into underperformance in key financial indicators (KFIs) it may be too late for management to identify the competitor.

The Game

The competitor that poaches market share under a zero-sum constraint is referred to throughout the book as the nearest rival. Zero-sum represents the simplest game, with a long history in game theory. In the classic two-player zero-sum game, one player wins by matching the other's action and the other wins by mismatching. In these circumstances we define management as players in a game wherein the marginal value of their action increases in the level of a competitor's action. This is the Edgeworth constraint, introduced more than 100 years ago by Edgeworth (1881) as the concept of complementarity. For example, the demand for cars increases the demand for petrol; or if Pfizer spend $10 million on research and development (R&D), competitors will do likewise and spend at least $10 million. Complementarities have an important connection with strategic situations (Vives, 2005), and in Framework $Tn=3$ the issue facing management is whether to follow a rival action or not. Zero-sum games allow us to model business strategy in an easily understood manner. However, they have been criticised as being not very helpful as a guide to prediction or decision making, partly because "equilibrium depends on strategic thinking and not learning" (Crawford and Iriberi, 2007, p. 1731).

In Framework $Tn=3$, observed learning is important in the sense that management observe actions as signals, but rather than update any prior beliefs about the action, management account for the signal and think that the competitor is likely to act if they want the competitor to act and think that the competitor is less likely to react if their action signals ambiguity that they will act, having been observed in the past as keeping to type. This is captured in Table 1.1 by the enviable coefficient E.

Table 1.1
Coefficient E: Envy/Entropy

n = 2	2 < n < 5
Zero-sum	Redistribution
Envy	Entropy

Zero-sum games facilitate an understanding of how players react to the zero-sum constraint. A fact finder observes that player A's market share increases because the market share of B is falling and unless A has the capacity (Chapter 5) to match the increased demand through time the market share gain will be elusive. However, if player A increases market share through its low pricing and B follows, then A and B enter a price matching sequence of price movements that could lead to a zero-price equilibrium.

The strategic interaction of prices relegates the importance of independent pricing; hence the players are faced with the paradox of tumbling price. The E coefficient falls within the bounds (0,1) such that as E decreases towards zero and the zero-sum constraint becomes more acute, envy can be ascribed to the behaviour of the player. As E increases towards 1, the redistribution of market shares can benefit one of two players in the market. Apple's iPhone has increased the market for mobile phones, and within that market there is a redistribution of market shares as a direct consequence of Apple's entry.

Management realise that competitors sometimes do things – reduce price or take costs out of production – that cannot be easily modelled. In Framework Tn=3, type of management is based on a range of variables that can be observed and computed by management, allowing them an opportunity to better understand rival management behaviour. However, in the game theory literature, 'differences of opinion arise in assessing the importance of preferences in explaining economic behaviour' (Samuelson, 2005, p. 495). So the proposed framework will draw upon the management models, the traditional Baumol model and the Marris model, and a cost leadership (CL) model. Later chapters will focus on a classification of types that can be drawn from non-cooperative game theory. Although specific economic characteristics will be identified – Baumol on price, Marris on dividends, CL on costs or leader-follower in game theory – our overall objective is to present a management framework within which management signal their type to the market.

The impact of both type and signalling on business strategy is the genesis of Framework Tn=3. Signals do convey information about type. A signal is the first derivative of type with respect to time allowing the observer of the signal to form a judgement on whether the information conveyed is true or false.

$$\text{Type} = f.(\text{Signals})$$

For example, if Baumol Inc conveys a signal in time period t and it is observed at t by Rival Inc, then Rival Inc can believe with certainty that Baumol Inc is of Baumol type and will be observed as reducing price to maximise revenues in time period t. Rival Inc can trust Baumol Inc, and trust in this particular instance becomes an assessment tool in Framework Tn=3. If they are competing for market share, then both Baumol Inc and Rival Inc are now in the market-as-a-game and they are both players in that game.

Arguably, type can be portrayed by a signal but not every signal observed portrays the truth about type. Baumol Inc can simultaneously signal a type and keep a secret. Rival Inc, a trusted competitor, will be in a preferred position if Rival Inc can read the signals from Baumol Inc and detect that secret. It is in reading the signals that an understanding of management type is crucial. Type as a value badge can therefore be a function of signals.

Strategy

Management behave strategically when they come to understand that each and every decision is followed by an action that is observed by the market participants. This gives us the strategy equation $S = PE + NP$. It is a combination of minimising the Penrose effect (see Chapter 2) and ensuring that one has a response to any reactions to one's initial decision in a game. The latter is known as the Nash premise (NP). Understanding strategy is at the cusp of business acumen, and Framework Tn = 3 explores the possibility that there are n = 3 supporting elements of a company's strategy set. A strategy set is a string of moves. Collectively, the three supporting elements define the strategy set, enabling a company to sustain or obtain a strategic advantage in the market. A company's ability or capability to obtain such an advantage depends on its status as a player in the market as a game.

Management are in a game when they abandon independent action, thus realising that there exists interdependence within the market that directly affects performance – not only profitability but also the sustainability of its strategic advantage and its conversion into a competitive advantage. The conversion requires knowledge of rivals and an ability to identify the nearest rival, as well as knowledge of the market in which the game is played. Management teams have many tools of analysis at their disposal. The new tools on display in this book focus on observed learning in a market where individual action has to do with the probability of a likely reaction from a competitor. Framing the action – to change price, to launch a new product or to invest in more R&D – is codependent on reading the signals from competitors in the market; observing their behaviour; and observing, identifying and finding patterns in the observed data. The initial point of analysis is to ascribe a critical timeline (CTL) to the market by converting the observed actions and reactions into a metric.

When Apple Inc launched its iPhone in early 2007, did it do so in the belief that there was a gPhone about to be launched in the market? Our conceptual analysis of **type** is reminiscent of the managerial models with an emphasis on management discretion within a company. The launch of any new product is a company secret. The exact timing is the prerogative of the CEO. The degree of discretion, however, will be influenced by signals in the market-as-a-game, underpinned by reference to the capacity constraints inherent in the production **technology** of the company. Time is introduced by the very nature of the game: in a sequential game each player has the **time** to observe the actions and reactions (the moves) of the opponent.

Collectively, type, technology and time represent Framework Tn=3. If the iPhone was launched at time period t because of signals about a gPhone, then the Apple Inc strategy can best be understood within Framework Tn=3. Likewise, in August 2009, Nokia signalled the pre-Christmas launch of a new laptop – the Booklet 3G, with both 3G and Wi-Fi capability – and Dell Inc is signalling entry into the smartphone market. Ironically, in the early 1990s there was speculation about a possible link between Dell Inc and Nokia in exploiting the complementarities in an evolving personal computer market. Strategy is about understanding the process of filtering the signals in the market. It has as much to do with avoiding a loss in market share as it has to do with gaining market share, playing to avoid losing rather than to win.

Traditional economic models, known as neoclassical profit maximisation models, are based on perfect knowledge and rational logic, aiming at maximising profit. The firm is defined as a single entity, with no separation of ownership and control, that seeks to maximise profit subject to resource and market constraints. While this has the advantage of being easy to model, it is relatively more difficult to model the importance of the decision-making process within the firm in how it affects the outcome of any decision. Conversely, the behavioural theories of Simon, for example, try to take into account that management, like any other human activity, is subject to the irrational, and is less focused on one single goal. The decision-making process allows the multiple decision makers in a firm to reach a satisfactory level of attainment towards their individual goals and involves a trade-off between each management group in their individual ambitions.

H.A. Simon (1958) introduces the notion of 'satisficing', a dilution of the absolute goal of maximising attainment given the limitation of knowledge and the degree of uncertainty that prevails on any given decision. Simon argues that "people possess limited cognitive ability and so can exercise only 'bounded rationality' when making decisions in complex, uncertain situations". This level of satisfaction is not fixed but varies depending on experience and perception of risk and uncertainty. This concept was developed by Cyert and March, who emphasise the "alternative decision logic – the logic of appropriateness, obligation, duty and rules". Thus, in most organisations, a set of standing instructions tends to dominate in most managerial decisions "rather than anticipatory, consequential choice".

Determining where the final decision rests is harder to model, as this varies from one organisation to another depending on how responsive the firm is to adjusting to their collective experience in the market-as-a-game. The outcome will also be influenced by the prevailing conditions surrounding decision making: Is it collective or individual, a sequence of choices or stand-alone, a single criterion or a collection of less-defined criteria, and how much is the inherent willingness within the management structure to obey the rules? By obeying the rules, management keep to type. Conversely, it may be argued that this adversarial approach to decision making can promote the dysfunctional creativity that Mary Follett espoused in *Creative Experience* (1924). Decisions that have been reached through this process of collective bargaining may be seen as having a greater chance of optimising the firm's resources and therefore its profitability. However, these multiple factors could also act as a constraint in achieving profit maximisation. Leibenstein, in *Beyond Economic Man* (1976), argue that x-factors could also dictate the behaviour and efficiency of the company. Depending on the firm's history of management initiatives, this x-inefficiency can affect the firm's productivity, profitability and size.

What Is Type?

Framework $Tn=3$ focuses on management as individuals; and, as individuals, management can be assessed or ranked by both personality and style, attributes that are personal, subjective, easily observed but difficult to determine. Management do have a unique idiosyncratic style of leadership. But there is a further intrinsic economic characteristic more meaningful as an innate determinant of a company's performance, and that we call 'type'. Type is a behavioural characteristic, often overt and occasionally covert, an innate characteristic that companies wish to observe as a barometer of the likely future behaviour of competitors in the delivery and execution of their strategy.

It is one thing to believe or think about how another individual is more likely to behave, and in the absence of any signals, chat or communication, one has to rely on one's belief system. Alternatively, management can observe behaviour as signals of likely action and identify patterns in the signals, as illustrated in Chapter 2.

For example, the Baumol hypothesis is about sales revenue maximisation, and one way to achieve this is to focus on price. Under normal circumstances, when price falls, consumers on average buy more and sales revenue should increase. Management can signal a Baumol type by focusing on price or by focusing on revenue maximisation. Since revenue maximisation can be achieved by using price, it becomes imperative for management to understand that price not only serves to maximise total revenue, but also acts as a signal to rival competitors. Organic growth, as opposed to growth by acquisition, is a key feature of the Marris model, with its emphasis on using capital for R&D expenditure in a trade-off with less dividends today for more dividends tomorrow. Management can signal a Marris type by focusing on organic growth by signalling increased R&D expenditure.

Later we will explore types that are located in non-cooperative game theory. For example, there is a type called 'price follower', wherein the management of company A are observed as reducing price in reaction to company B's price movement. What, if anything, can the management of company B infer from the behaviour of company A? What, if anything, can they glean from additional information on type? If company A's type is signalled as a price follower type, and if that type has particular attributes, what guarantees do company B's management have that the management of company A will subscribe to them at a given point in time? In particular, would they necessarily follow company B's price lead in a game?

In the market-as-a-game, management wait and observe what happens. Because the future is not certain, the probability that reaction from rivals will follow a certain company's action will be very high in some markets, notably in the oligopoly markets, where interdependence is the norm. The value of waiting thus increases. Management that would have hithertofore acted unilaterally on a product launch (Marris type) or price change (Baumol type) may reconsider their plans. In the interim, rivals observe each other in a wait-and-see scenario. Why is the future not certain? There are many reasons advanced in the management literature; here we focus specifically on three – type, technology and time, or Framework Tn=3.

Trade-offs

In order to understand types of management we need to understand trade-offs. An indifference relationship considers the trade-off between two variables, X and Y. Management type can be linked to a financial variable – profits, costs, value or sales revenue. For example, a Baumol type of management focuses on revenues and sales maximisation, a Marris type focuses on organic growth through product diversification, and a price follower focuses on competitive price movements. Therefore, one key determinant in understanding management type is the ability to unravel the trade-off that is implicit in the management's decision making. In other words, we need to identify a third variable, Z, about which variables X and Y are indifferent because Z remains constant over the decision-making horizon.

The family of management models, including Baumol, the early models of Williamson and indeed Marris, have two key attributes in common, attributes that park their application outside the traditional range of the microeconomic theory of the firm. First, management are not so preoccupied with profit maximisation as is the norm within the neoclassical models of the firm. There are other variables that attract the interest of management – maximising revenue, maximising the growth of the company, avoiding price wars, or indeed maximising their personal utility or satisfaction. It is the latter that gives rise to a second distinguishing characteristic of the management models – the application of indifference curve analysis to management behaviour.

Indifference Analysis

Within the neoclassical paradigm the indifference analysis is uniquely applied to understanding the behaviour of consumers: the random consumers are said to be indifferent between two baskets of fruit if their utility – the Z or third variable – does not change when choosing one basket over another. So whether the consumers have five apples and three oranges or three apples and five oranges, their utility does not change, and thus they are declared indifferent between both baskets of fruit. An indifference relationship can be ascribed to their choice. However, we are presented with a unique application when we ascribe an indifference analysis to the behaviour of management.

We need to identify two variables around which management could be indifferent: profits and market share, or profits and annualised sales revenues. The choice of pair may be entirely subjective, as managements differ in their trade-offs across the variables. For some managements intent on lowering costs, there may be a trade-off between labour and capital expenditures, with a shift between less labour-intensive and more capital-intensive production technology, provided productivity does not change. In such a scenario, productivity takes the place of utility – a third parameter that does not change as management decide between the pairs of less L more K, and more L less K. The difficulty lies in identifying that elusive third variable, a difficulty compounded by the subjective nature of the indifference analysis. In the Marris model, however, we will identify value as marked by the market capitalisation of a company, as a candidate for the third variable, but value that is underpinned by growth.

Z or Third Variable

It is in trying to identify a third variable that type becomes important in understanding management behaviour, since type can be signalled to competitors by the observed behaviour of management. As individuals we are inclined to keep to type, indicated by our behaviour as we keep to type. It is these patterns of observed behaviour that companies should be looking for in scoping the behaviour of the management of a competitor. For example, if a new CEO has a history of growing companies by acquisition, then there is a high probability that the CEO will keep to type in the new company and attempt to grow by acquisition rather than achieving organic growth.

Detecting the identity of the third variable, Z, is interesting. Remember that management are prepared to trade off Y and X only if U(Z) does not change. So what is Z? This is a guessing game between management and the investment community, shareholders and external stakeholders, including competitors. The identity of Z could provide an insight into the strategic thinking of the management, and that becomes critical in the playing of games. Figure 1.1 illustrates a managerial indifference trade-off relationship.

**Figure 1.1
Management Indifference**

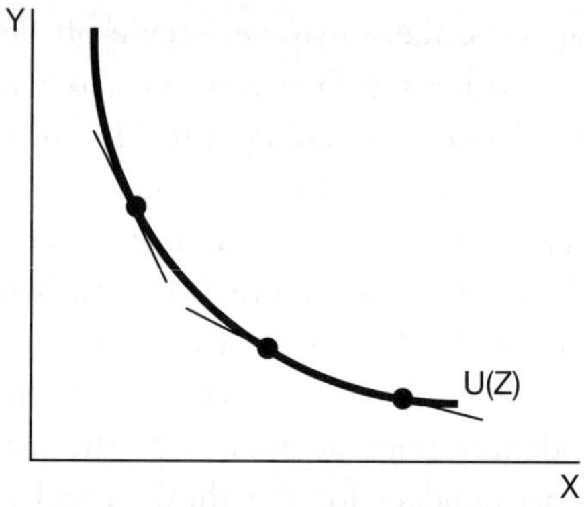

[Figure: Indifference curve U(Z) plotted with Y on vertical axis and X on horizontal axis, convex to the origin, with two tangent points marked.]

Often, Z is identified by management as growth, value or costs. But generally it is camouflaged. Management do provide signals to the market, or investment commentators and analysts contribute to the guessing game by offering opinions as to the identity of Z. We shall look in detail at the Marris model, wherein managerial discretionary behaviour is allowed because of the principal-agent relationship that facilitates growth. Management, therefore, have the discretion to focus on the growth rate of a firm. By adjusting the growth rate, management can achieve their personal goals, such as status, power and pay.

Premium on Type

We can ascribe an indifference relationship to management type. The explanatory power of a managerial indifference relationship is greatly enhanced when we include forms of personal and social capital in the management utility function. Management receive share options, and indeed the share price of a company includes a premium on the type of CEO. In Apple's case, for example, there is a premium on Steve Jobs as CEO built into the share price. Management have objectives, and they derive a sense of personal satisfaction from realising those objectives. An important attribute is that type displays signals to the market inclusive of consumers and competitors. More important, the signals are observed by shareholders and investors in the company. There are two important signals: (a) dividends signal and (b) price signal. The latter is crucial in that we have elevated price to the level of signal. What does that mean? Traditionally, if company A lowers its price, it is in reaction to a level of demand. Now, that very act of lowering price may be construed by a competitor as a threat to their sales and thus provoke a price reaction. One must remember that 50p is cheap if the competitor is 60p; but reducing one's price to 30p will secure more sales only if the competitor is still 60p.

Positive Learning Transfer

In our observations there are different time periods – t – which corresponds to now, and the future as represented by time period t+1. Decisions taken in time period t have consequences in time period t+1. In other words, a trade-off between two variables in time period t could be explained by the likely impact of that trade-off on a third variable in time period t+1. Consider the following scenario. Growth in a company depends upon growth in the market. In the market the company sells a range of products, so growth in the products will grow the market. Product diversification at time period t enables the company to grow organically in t+1. However, this requires investment in R&D and technology to ensure that the products are differentiated in the market to sustain the growth in sales required to filter back into company growth.

With higher investment in R&D there may be a claim on the finances of the company in time period t, as shareholders require dividends; as more is expended on R&D, the company may go to the external market to borrow funds. Alternatively, management may decide to use internal funds to finance the R&D in period t, postpone dividend payments until period t+1 and focus on maximising the growth of the company. As the company grows, and management opt to deliver dividends in period t+1, the value of the company may increase. This implicit trade-off observed in a Marris type, between payment of dividends versus more expenditure on R&D, is at the heart of understanding the Marris model. The elusive third variable is the value of the company.

Table 1.2
Model Objectives

	Behavioural	Baumol	Marris	Framework Tn=3
Objective	Multiple goals	Sales	Growth	Z or 3rd variable
Approach	Satisficing – subject to profit constraint	Maximisation – subject to profit constraint	Maximisation – subject to security constraint	Maximisation – subject to external constraints
Principal-Agent Relationship	Yes	Yes	Yes	Yes
Short vs. Long Term	Varies	Short	Long	Time period t+1
Reaction & Interaction	Yes	Partial	Yes	Nash replies
Decision-making Coalitions	Yes	No	No	DQs

How can an optimal trade-off be achieved? It can be achieved by a **positive learning transfer** (PLT) from the management to the shareholders, orchestrated by providing information and reassurance in the activities of management. And, of course, if management have been observed in the past as successfully maximising growth, then shareholders may be persuaded to trust the type of management.

However, shareholders are prone to follow a Bayesian-type rule in seeing what they want to see; so if profits fall in time period t, during the refocus of strategy towards more product diversification, shareholders will only see the falling profits and react by selling stock. It is therefore imperative for management to transfer a positive learning about their behaviour and plans to the shareholders. This can explain the willingness of many CEOs to appear on business channels such as cnbc.com and Bloomberg.com.

Behavioural Approach

One of the more interesting applications in the business world is the application of game theory in shaping strategy. Game theory focuses on observed behaviour and allows us to identify patterns from which we can predict a likely future outcome. Look around you: observe the number of right-handed people you encounter. It is relatively easy to predict that if you were to hand anybody a pen, they would write with their right hand. However, if the individuals know that you are observing them as right-handed individuals, then some of them may try to fool you and write using their left hands. A game of poker is a typical game of observation and trust wherein a sequence of moves is played, the game ends, and then winnings or pay-offs are realised. The sequence of poker hands can be regarded as moves, and they represent a game. Schooled players look for connections between poker hands, and each player observes what every other player does or does not do as the game unfolds. Every day in the business world, management observe rival prices, costs and share price movements. The business environment is one that is rich with observed data.

While all these managerial models recognise and promote a single overriding goal that complements profit maximisation, they are all in their own way forced to recognise that other factors can potentially interfere with the model. This would imply that focusing on a single overriding goal is unrealistic. The behaviourist approach recognises the multiplicity of goals from these managerial models and allows for the greater complexity that results by moving away from a single 'maximised' result to a 'satisficed' result. It is the means by which an outcome is reached – not the goal – that is important, because the outcome is a compromise on many different goals, the influence and importance of each varying from one business to another.

Therefore, management display certain characteristics – a type – depending on their business and industry experience, the costs and the constraints of competition. Over time, management's objective is to increase the relative performance of the company, and Framework $Tn=3$ conceptually integrates the core of economic reasoning with the other business disciplines, for example, finance and marketing, by providing a common framework for investigating and understanding management behaviour as a signalling game. Management behaviour expands with the market-as-a-game or disappears as a function of the game. In the real world, business decisions may be influenced by many different considerations. The owners and managers of firms may have a variety of goals and objectives, especially over longer periods of time. They may conceivably be motivated by a desire to become well respected in the community, or to serve some other higher purpose such as promoting their home country's national objectives, or they may simply want their organisation to become as large and powerful as possible. However, the basic economic theory of business behaviour is based on a very different premise: that firms exist to earn profits and that the goal of management is to maximise those profits (or minimise their losses) in time period $t+1$.

Framework $Tn=3$ places emphasis on explaining how decisions are taken within the firm, and goes well beyond neoclassical economics. In our earlier reference to the Baumol hypothesis, if management opt for a price reduction in order to increase total revenue, the objective will depend ultimately on the price reaction of the competitor. Thus, management type, player type and different choice situations call for different decision approaches by management. Completely rational decision making involves identifying alternatives, projecting the probabilities and outcomes of alternatives, and evaluating the outcomes according to known preferences. These information-gathering and information-processing requirements are beyond the capabilities of any organisation. In practice, organisational decision making departs from the rational ideal in important ways depending on the contingencies of the decision context. Cyert and March (1963) coupled bounded rationality with the assumption that human actors are myopic.

Therefore, the behaviour of management is critically assessed in the context of testing management's ability to affect outcomes. Management as an individual is to be understood in terms of a rational individual making a decision. Within the decision-making process for a modern organisation, management teams take actions according to how their combined effort and expertise impact on knowing when and how to act. The conflict – that is, the trade-off – referred to earlier is necessarily a conflict of subjective outcomes, as different managements have different outcomes in a given action. Management A, for example, change price to achieve a subjective outcome; however, management B's reaction to the price change will depend on B's own subjective outcome. Neither of the managements take price as exogenous. Price is now a signal. Therefore, both A and B need to know all the types of participants in the market as well as their own firm's production technology in order to compete.

CHAPTER 2

Game Embedded Strategy

> "We are capable of continuing to believe things that all the evidence shows not to be true, even long after everyone has demonstrated that they're not true."
>
> *George Orwell*

The original neoclassical theory of the firm was developed on the assumption of perfect knowledge. That assumption has now been substantially modified, and its modification has allowed the development of sophisticated theories of decision making under conditions of uncertainty. But this uncertainty relates simply to the future outcome of alternative courses of action; and it is uncertainty of a probabilistic kind. But uncertainty extends much wider than this. Management are bounded rational – they do not have the information that traditional theory assumes they have. They are information-constrained, or the information may be flawed or out-of-date. Therefore, strategy needs to be defined within the contours of bounded rationality.

In addition, the market is a game, as rival competitors compete for market share. Each move by a company can be observed, and a sequence of moves constitutes a strategy. Type, for the purposes of this book, refers to the boundary of managerial behaviourism, that is, the study of management's covert behaviour. As applied to management in understanding strategy, there is a need to focus on the role of subjective value and methodological individualism, that is, management as individuals realising their wills despite the resistance of others. In other words, the CEO is an individual and management are individuals; and as individuals they have a type. Views on type and related topics have deep historical roots across many disciplines in an attempt to understand the behaviour of rational action (T. Jones, 2004; Mahoney, 2005; R. Hagstrom, 2005).

Companies are players in a game, and the game dimensions are defined in terms of geography and product. So we have some interesting observations: Nokia entering the US market in smartphones, or Dell entering the market for smartphones, or Apple evolving as a smartphone player. Each observation is defined in terms of the geography and the product in which the game will be played. The observations are transferred to a critical timeline (CTL) that allows the observer to find a pattern in the observed points. The game begins upon the action of one player – observed as a price decrease. A second player reacts in a match-match sequence of price movements over a time period. The strategy question is framed in terms of two related issues: What did the player who initiated the price decrease believe about the likely reaction from the competitor? How long will both players, observed in a sequence of matching price moves, continue to match each other's price movements? The first question speaks to the belief system of each player, and the second speaks to the concept of a Nash equilibrium.

Critical Timeline

The key to understanding management type in Framework $Tn=3$ is to understand behaviour, and thus to infer from observed behaviour the likely actions and reactions of management in the business world. Management can suffer from a failure to understand competitor behaviour. Part of the explanation is that management are bounded rational; in other words, they do not factor in all the possible scenarios, nor do they put in the time and effort to analyse rival behaviour, clinging instead to a bunker silo approach. At the root of this failure is a misunderstanding of the importance of type. If management's decision to do x is in any way influenced by the type of rival management, then competitors do have an implicit belief system, thinking or believing what the other may do or how they may act.

It is one thing to believe or think about how another individual is more likely to behave; and in the absence of any signals, chat or communication, one has to rely on one's belief system. Alternatively, management can observe behaviour as signals and as patterns in the signals. The pattern can be difficult to determine and requires many years of observations. In the interim, we can read the signals of CEO type by listening to their views on cnbc.com or Bloomberg.com, at conferences or at company briefings to the equity markets. Each CEO has a type, a particular economic characteristic that can give a clue to strategy. It is imperative to observe the signals in order to understand type. Patterns do emerge in the observed behaviour, patterns on price movements or patterns to do with achieving growth through acquisition. The patterns create a critical timeline (CTL) of observed actions and as the CTL unfolds, it reveals a strategy (see Figure 2.1). McNutt (2008) discusses the CTL for Microsoft and Sony during the period 2000 to 2004 with the launch of PS2 and Xbox. Comparing CTLs for Nissan and General Motors can help in evaluating the strategy adopted at Nissan. Refer to the CTL for Nokia and Apple on page 92 (Figure 7.3).

**Figure 2.1
Critical Timeline: Nissan**

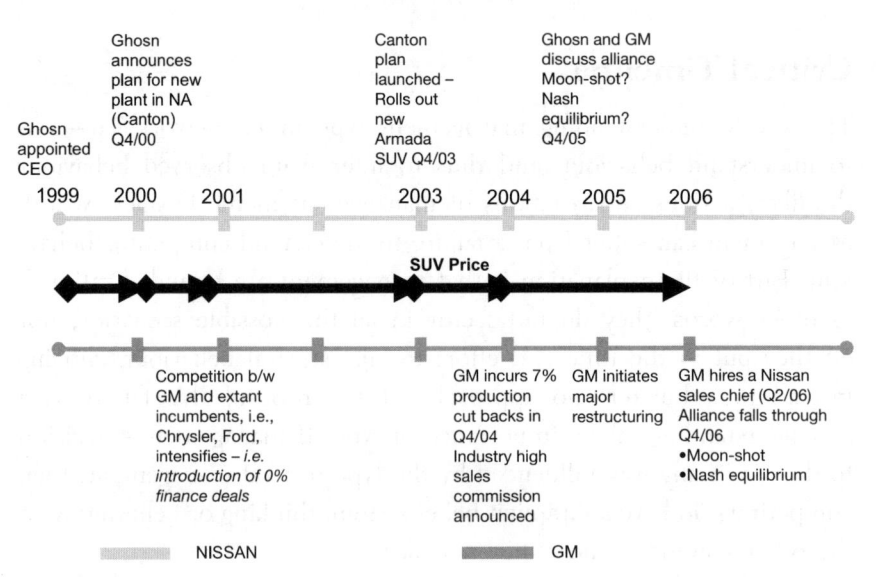

Ghosn appointed CEO	Ghosn announces plan for new plant in NA (Canton) Q4/00			Canton plan launched – Rolls out new Armada SUV Q4/03		Ghosn and GM discuss alliance Moon-shot? Nash equilibrium? Q4/05	
1999	2000	2001		2003	2004	2005	2006

SUV Price

	Competition b/w GM and extant incumbents, i.e., Chrysler, Ford, intensifies – *i.e.* introduction of 0% finance deals		GM incurs 7% production cut backs in Q4/04 Industry high sales commission announced	GM initiates major restructuring	GM hires a Nissan sales chief (Q2/06) Alliance falls through Q4/06 •Moon-shot •Nash equilibrium

NISSAN   GM

Zero-sum Constraint

In the competitive environment known as oligopoly, wherein there are five or fewer rival competitors, a degree of interdependence arises in the market. Interdependence creates a game dimension and transforms management into players. Therefore, it behoves us to look at both management type and player type, reserving the latter term to describe the behaviour of firms, that is, firms and companies as we have come to understand them in modern business. In the case of Intel versus AMD in microprocessors, the gain in market share by one competitor is at the expense of the other, as they both try to gain increasing market share or consolidate existing shares. In many markets a unilateral gain in market share can occur as a direct consequence of a loss accruing to a competitor.

The zero-sum constraint also acts as an external constraint. Once management realise that their pricing and output decisions depend as much on the likely reactions of competitors as they do on understanding their consumers, management may have to understand that there is a price and quantity output that is the best they can achieve given the likely reactions of the competitors. It is not, however, the best they can achieve in terms of their own motives. This is the Nash premise (see Figure 2.2), to which we will return in a later chapter.

The zero-sum constraint can easily arise in product markets where there are fickle preferences and changing demand for increasingly differ-

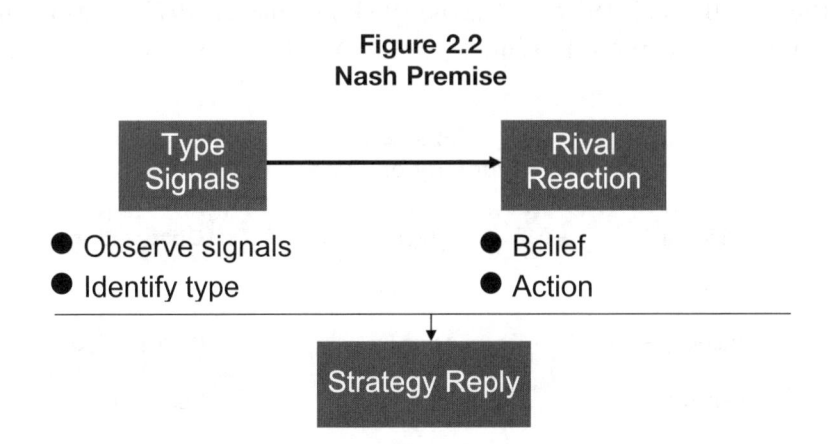

**Figure 2.2
Nash Premise**

Type Signals → Rival Reaction

- Observe signals
- Identify type

- Belief
- Action

Strategy Reply

entiated products amongst consumers. A player can lag behind in the market due to an inability to differentiate fast enough. This is contrary to the Model-T effect: Consumers will buy a Model-T – available only in the colour black – but over time, preferences will change and more consumers will buy different brands of coloured cars. Growth and discretionary theories such as Marris and Baumol formally start from the same point that management have power over an objective function. Included in a managerial objective function are the motives of management: a desire for sustainable long-term growth in the size of the company as measured by (say) assets, employees, output or market share. In managerial theories, the pursuit of managerial motives is subject to external shareholder constraint. The motives of management reveal their type.

Penrose Effect

The real-world competitive environment is different from the textbook model of the perfectly competitive economy. In a perfectly competitive market, product markets are assumed to be supplied by a large number of small single-plant, single-product, owner-managed price-taking firms with limited, if any, capacity for growth. Economists began responding to this from the mid-1950s to the mid-1970s, responses that can now be placed into three distinct groups: discretionary theories (Baumol, 1959; Williamson, 1970); growth-oriented theories (Penrose, 1958; Marris, 1964; Mueller, 1972); and bureaucratic theories (Monsen and Downs, 1965; W. Baumol, 1959; R. Marris, 1964; D. Mueller, 1972; R. Monsen and A. Downs, 1965; E. Penrose, 1958; O. Williamson, 1970).

Table 2.1
Typology on Type

Signal	Type	Observation
Price	Baumol	Low prices
Dividends	Marris	R&D increase
Costs	CL	Reduce costs

The modern company is a bureaucratic structure with an administrative system that could frustrate the achievement of sustainable growth. Consequently, there are unique internal constraints within each company. The management operate within this structure; problems may arise within the management team on information about opportunities for growth, or top management may not be capable of making a decision. In other words, management per se may act as a constraint on achieving a growth rate through time. This is referred to as the Penrose effect, and it represents a tangible cost of growth within the company. It is the failure to understand type and its implications that exacerbates the Penrose effect. It is imperative for management to realise that their respective actions are interdependent. Once management recognise their interdependence and act accordingly, then they are in what we label a game dimension. How to incorporate the rival's type into the decision on x will be guided by the rules of sequential non-cooperative games; how best to respond will ultimately depend on the underlying cost and production technology of the company.

Nash Premise

In the game dimension there is an important rule. It is called the Prisoners' Dilemma (PD). It is critical for management to understand the dilemma in order to avoid incurring a Penrose effect. In the original PD two prisoners are faced with a dilemma when caught by the police for burglaries: do they trust each other enough to cooperate to minimise total loss of liberty, or will one of them, trusting the other to cooperate, betray her so as to go free? Knowing that there is a bond of trust, the police interview each prisoner separately and tell each prisoner that the other has informed on them. So does each prisoner trust her friend, or does she betray the friend and take the deal from the police? Both prisoners betray in the absence of a strong bond of trust. The strategy of betrayal or confession is defined as a dominant strategy, the best (or worst), regardless of how the rival plays.

The winnings or pay-offs are determined by the components of the market-as-a-game. The game occurs once an action leads to a reaction. It is a measure of strategic advantage if management have anticipated the likely reaction, and thus are not surprised by the reaction. The key parameters in this game include rival management type, which can be observed by signals from senior management. Equally important is to deduce how one's type is perceived by one's competitors in the market-as-a-game.

The application of game theory in general to management and business is very important, particularly in a zero-sum market wherein two or three firms collectively have 100 per cent of the market share (Nalebuff, 2008; Baye, 2008; Nalebuff, 2008. This is the classic oligopoly market structure, in which the players recognise their mutual independence. A strategy set is a sequence of moves. A sequence could be composed of a move either to cooperate or to compete. Competition policy and antitrust rules exist in many jurisdictions in order to dissuade firms from forming a credible cartel arrangement. Cartels are inherently unstable, because of an incentive to cheat. Modern companies do compete by cooperating through joint ventures, technology sharing and outsourcing. In an oligopoly market with five players, the presence of an acute zero-sum constraint and interdependence can act as a trigger for a merger wave in the industry. In other words, once management realise that they are players and the market shapes the dimension of the game, an alternative to competing is simply to cooperate or merge. But there is always the element of trust.

If the players trust each other, then they can believe the signals in the market. However, there is still a preference for dishonesty amongst some players, and thus it becomes critical to understand the type of player in the game. Chandler's thesis is that structure follows strategy. In other words, it is the behaviour of management, observed in the CTL as strategy by competitors, that determines the market structure. If a firm's strategy is to be carried out, or implemented, individuals working within the firm must know about the strategy and its operational requirement for tasks and actions. How management respond to problems of information, innovation, coordination and commitment in a game will determine its long-term position in that game. How they respond to problems of information, innovation, coordination and commitment in a market-as-a-game will determine the firm's long-term position in an industry.

What Market Should We Be In?

It is critical for management to answer the question "What market should we be in?" (See Figure 2.3.) A company should not be in a market-as-a-game unless they understand the dimensions of the game, that is, the number of players and the type of each of the players in the game.

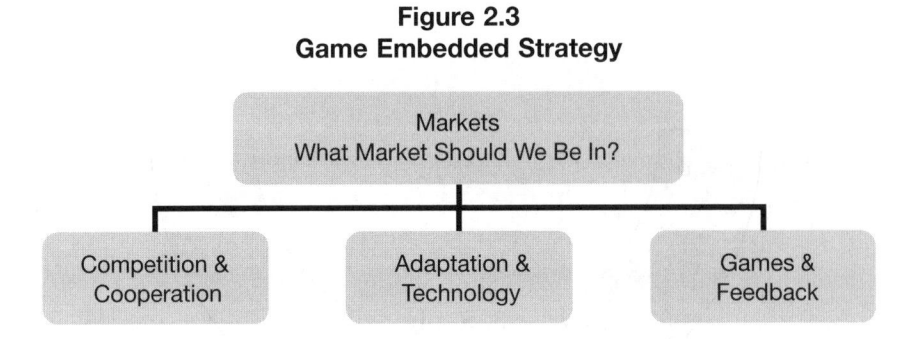

**Figure 2.3
Game Embedded Strategy**

```
                    Markets
          What Market Should We Be In?
         /            |              \
Competition &    Adaptation &      Games &
Cooperation      Technology        Feedback
```

The decision-making process involves a choice between three possible scenarios: (1) competition and cooperation, (2) adaptation, and (3) technology and game and feedback. Determining what market the company should be in is hard, as this will vary from one firm to another depending on the influence that management are able to exercise – on management type, on player type and on how responsive shareholders are to adjusting management expectations. The outcome will also be influenced by the decision-making process per se within the firm and the inherent willingness to follow the rules. Once management discount the likely reaction of a competitor to an impending price change, management are said to be in a 'game' wherein decisions and outcomes are interdependent. The degree of interdependence is important: as the number of competitors falls below five (oligopoly) there is a mutual understanding driven by the innate structure of the market that each company in an oligopoly structure could do better in the absence of price competition. It is a different matter to announce that management proceed to cooperate: on the contrary, we begin from the premise of non-cooperation.

**Figure 2.4
The Wheel of Belief**

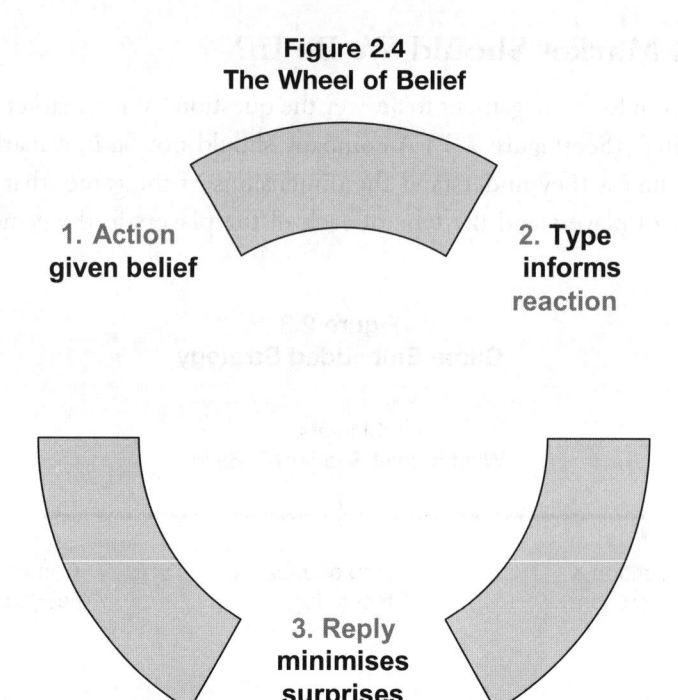

1. Action
given belief

2. Type
informs
reaction

3. Reply
minimises
surprises

In a GEMS environment of non-cooperation with mutual interdependence, a decision by company A will lead to a reaction from company B. Therefore, A should expect a reaction from B and vice versa. If the management of company A have no contingency in terms of any reaction from B, then there is the possibility of misguided decision making by A. The expectation of a likely reaction and its computation is at the heart of the economics of strategy. The economics of strategy contains an emphasis on the use of non-cooperative game theory as a tool of analysis to understand management behaviour. Careful attention is given to management type and the identification of signals from the decisions, actions and commentary of management. Decisions on price and costs, for example, are taken in the context of likely reaction from competitors.

Critical Timeline and Ambush Strategy

In Cross's book, *Jungle Warfare* (1989), there is an interesting discussion of military ambush strategy during World War II. According to Cross, ambushes can be of any shape, but basically they are linear and covers a geographical area. The critical timeline (CTL) is a linear concept and allows management to identify a pattern of observed behaviour. The geography and the product spaces define the dimensions of the game. The author continues to identify the parameters for success: "For success a few things not to be forgotten on the battlefield: surprise, silence, security, a rehearsal whenever possible and a reserve" (p. 211). Earlier in his book, he argues that an adverse reaction on being surprised can be minimised by well-tried and instinctive immediate action drills. But there are signals, as indicated in this passage on tracking discipline: "One successful alternative was leaving the track walking backwards into the jungle with some of the force continuing walking forwards then leaving the track into the jungle on the opposite side… [sic]; this was risky as the footprint of those walking backwards (when the toe imprint is greater) and those walking forwards (when the heel imprint is greater) are patently obvious" (p. 87). The linearity is captured by the CTL, which tracks a range of observations, including price and product specifications.

The area dimension of ambush strategy is about geography. In China in late 2008, a company called Tencent emerged as a leading player in the instant text messaging (IM) market, ahead of MSN. Tencent's QQ instant messaging success was linked to the demand for IM from the young, newly employed Chinese consumers. The threat from the new 3G cellular networks offering more Chinese consumers access to mobile email will appear on the horizon in 2009–2010 as 3G networks begin to roll out their services. How should Tencent react? One possibility is to adopt a 'well-tried and instinctive immediate action drill': QQ's success is based on the social networking and online gaming services it provides. So it could 'walk forward' into a strategy that builds on these two aspects with a range of functionalities that are better than those currently available on tried and tested 3G networks abroad.

CHAPTER 3

Baumol Hypothesis

> "Ah, but I was so much older then,
> I'm younger than that now."
>
> *Bob Dylan*

In the history of economics applied to the business world, many scholars and practitioners were sceptical about the focus on managerial behaviour. During the latter half of the 20th century, managerial theories of the firm began to emerge in the literature as economic theories on how the behaviour of modern management affected the working of the economic system, rather than the other way around. The debate on strategy determining structure is implicit in the Chicago hypothesis of modern antitrust, and the Chandler dilemma is a key component of strategic management. They have, however, been the subject of considerable research in the management literature.

This book is not about the models per se; however, some of the managerial models will inform our discussion of type. As suggested, Baumol type is related to the fundamentals of the Baumol model: there is a correlation between price and total revenue, depending on the price elasticity of demand. When a price reduction is observed, rival management should stop and think: is it a one-shot price reduction to increase total revenue or not? How rival management respond depends on their belief system and on what they observe as signals in the market.

So type is ascribed to management as a unique, and sometimes idiosyncratic, behavioural characteristic that can be inferred from understanding the motives of management. Arguably, management in debates over strategy can look to behavioural theories about type to gain a better appreciation of the assumptions and foundations of their own business acumen. For type to be relevant to understanding modern business, we will argue throughout that outcomes, as measured by key financial indicators, are equally likely across management but that information about a competitor's management type delivers a competitive advantage.

Oligopoly n < 5

Five is the key number of competitors (n) in a market. With five or fewer competitors, each competitor becomes increasingly aware of the degree of mutual interdependence amongst the group. Framework $Tn=3$ could provide management with a framework for assessing the competitive environment in markets increasingly defined by a smaller number of competing firms. How small? Markets are increasingly characterised by five or fewer rival competitors, the quintessential oligopoly market structure. In everyday experience, management as a team are concerned with price and quantity outcomes in an oligopoly market and how those outcomes could change from one particular circumstance to another in that competitive environment. For example, the appointment of a new chief executive officer by a rival could change the outcomes and indeed the dimensions of the game.

In the literature, dissatisfaction with the simple conception of a firm as a mechanism that transforms atomistic inputs into marketable outputs has resulted in alternative perspectives on the firm. New emphasis has been placed on the internal structure of the corporate firm, and the emerging managerial theory emphasises the complex nature of the modern corporate firm. In their pioneering work, Berle and Means (1932) describe the diminishing influence of shareholders in the decision-making process of large corporations in the United States from the turn of the 20th century. This left much of the decision making to management, whose objectives, it was suggested, could be different from those of the owners of the firm. If, in terms of its influence on managers' salaries, size of firm, for example, was more important than firms' profitability, then growth could be a more important objective of firms than profit. This is the key to unlocking the third variable.

Other reasons were advanced as to why management may be more preoccupied by sales or revenue maximisation than by profit maximisation (Baumol, 1967). If sales fail to rise, this is often equated with reduced market share and market power, and, consequently, with increased vulnerability to the actions of competitors. Under a zero-sum constraint, management may not realise their sales targets as rivals poach market share. When asked about the way his company performs, an executive would typically reply in terms of what the firm's levels of sales are. The financial market and retail distributors are more responsive to a firm with rising sales. The model developed by Baumol attempts to reconcile the behavioural conflict between profit maximisation and the maximisation of the firm's sales, its total revenue. It assumes that the firm maximises sales revenue subject to a minimum profit constraint.

Elasticity

The revenue-maximising level of output is the level at which the marginal revenue is 0 and the elasticity of demand is 1. For a Baumol total, revenue sales maximising firm prices are low when demand is elastic, that is, for every 10 per cent reduction in price, total revenue would increase by at least 10 per cent. Embedded in the demand relationship is a measurement of how responsive demand is to price changes. This is called price elasticity, ϵp. It is a key link between price and total revenue. A supplier will supply more if the price increases, subject to production constraints. However, at the higher price with greater supply, a key question remains: Is the total revenue accruing from the additional supply higher than before the price change? This goes to the heart of the concept of elasticity, which measures the responsiveness of demand to price.

$$\epsilon p = \%\Delta q / \%\Delta p$$

Remember that the formula for total revenue (TR) is TR = p.q. So any change in TR can come about from either a price change $\%\Delta p$ or a change in demand (at a given price) $\%\Delta q$.

The q is the amount of product purchased by the normal rational consumer. For some products, if the price increases, then TR will increase. There are products for which TR will increase only if the price actually falls. The former are inelastic products, and the latter are elastic products – the key driver is the responsiveness of demand to price changes. This is clearly illustrated later in this chapter.

Baumol Type

A Baumol type focuses on pricing as a driver of revenue and volumes but may face a cost-volume constraint, whereas a Marris type chooses between maximum dividends or growth but faces shareholder concerns over the value of the company. Competitors would observe a Baumol-type strategy based on leveraging revenues from a pricing policy. Provided demand is sufficiently elastic, a price reduction should produce the increase in intended sales revenue. It is by reducing price that management are able to maximise revenue yield from the asset. This is better known in the industry as yield per passenger, average revenue per user (ARPU) or simply 'bums on seats' pricing.

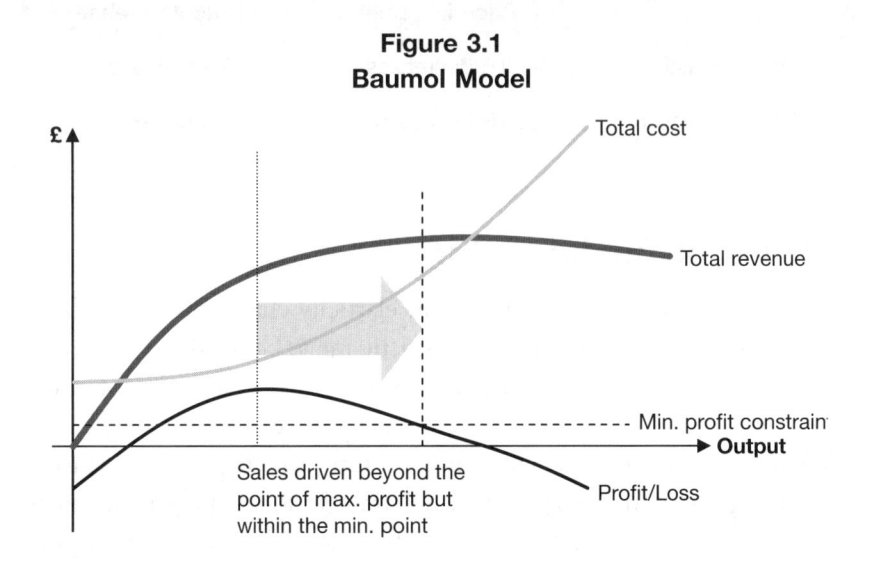

**Figure 3.1
Baumol Model**

The business model works until elasticity falls: initially elasticity is high as consumers switch from good or service x to the Baumol good or service y, but the preference set of the once-x-now-y consumers changes as they experience the good but with lower opportunity costs. These are known as switching costs. To understand this, recall that the revenue is TR = p.q and that ΔTR = Δp.q is to be followed by Δq at the new lower p, Δp. There is a sequence in pricing as revenue awaits the lag in quantity-sales response. For various reasons, particularly to do with quality and price, consumers may be weary of a price reduction from the higher priced elastic segment. In that segment, the higher prices have been sustained and supported probably by increased advertising and consumer persuasion. Or the Δq may not materialise as consumers remain loyal to a rival player, or indeed, even with Δp = 8, the final lower price may still be higher relative to a rival's price. So Baumol pricing, favoured by the low-cost airlines model of revenue yield management, would fit into the top right-hand corner of Table 3.1.

Table 3.1
Total Revenue Test

	Price Increase	Price Decrease
Ep > 1 Elastic	TR decreases	TR increases
Ep < 1 Inelastic	TR increases	TR decreases

Paradox of Tumbling Price

There is a trigger price, at which point elasticity changes from an elastic range above the trigger price to an inelastic range below the trigger price (see Figure 3.2). At the trigger price ep = 1. It is significant because it determines the total revenue response to any price change. Consider the following example: if the current price is 40p and a trigger price is to be computer-generated at 31p, it will be strategic for management not to proceed with a 10p reduction in price, because at 30p the reduced price

**Figure 3.2
Trigger Price**

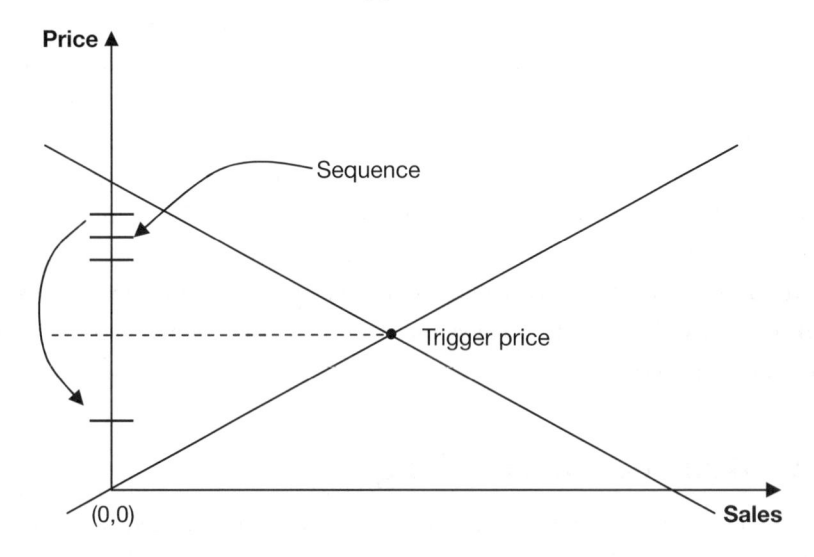

is less than the trigger price: 30p < 31p. Instead, a price reduction of less than 9p (no more than 8p) would fall within the trigger price boundary constraint, and as price falls from 40p to 32p, revenue should increase under the total revenue test. The trigger price can complement the mark-up price P > AVC and the net margin price P > AC, where AVC is average variable cost and AC is the total average cost.

Sales Fuel Profits

The paradox can be overcome by price positioning with different prices at different times for different consumers. The paradox adds to the complexity of what price to charge by raising the issue of how much the reduction or increase in price should be. That belies the fact that management would always wish to reduce price, outside the remit of price wars, price promotion and price discrimination. Conversely, increasing price from a relatively lower base requires sufficient spend on advertising to ensure that that segment of the demand function complies with inelasticity. Empirical evidence has concluded that increased advertising expenditure rescues the elasticity of demand less than 1, but this applies to the entire range of the demand and refers to the overall slope of the demand (Schmalensee, 1979). In the segment, management should think of the low price as a penetration price strategy, and once price is well below a trigger price, only then should a price increase be considered. And if advertising expense is increased, the lower segment encroaches more of the entire demand. In other words, an inelastic entire demand will have a greater probability of inelastic segments. It is important for management in general to realise that sales revenue growth (ΔTR) adjusted for market growth represents **market share gain**. Essentially, management are creating demand as well as building a brand.

Mr Mun and Mr Hotelling

One strategy to achieve sales revenue growth can be located in mercantilist theories attributable to Mr Mun. According to Mun's strategy, a product enters the market at a lower price, market share is cultivated, and then, only then, should price increase, ensuring a small but insignificant drop in sales revenue. This strategy is better known in marketing as 'penetration pricing'. If a trigger price is high, because of the low level of elasticity, then management should consider positioning the product's price at the higher end of the price scale and, in effect, be dissuaded from reducing price. In the latter case, even with the poaching of market share by generic products, branded products should distance their price as far away as allowed by the boundaries of the trigger price from the relatively lower priced generic.

This line of argument accords with an interpretation of Hotelling's maximal differentiation principle. And as an intermediary price strategy, price discrimination should be considered as a deliberate non-price war attempt to offer consumers a range of prices for the same product. First-degree discrimination requires arbitrage and negotiation and is more appropriate for the pricing of services. For example, in holding on to clients' accounts, advertising executives may engage in this form of pricing. But it is the second and third degrees that should interest the discerning strategic player. With second-degree pricing, volume discounts, as well as coupon pricing and the 'six-pack phenomenon', are offered. Under third-degree pricing, depending on how the market is fragmented, different prices could be charged to different consumers at different times of day. Ironically, third-degree pricing allows management to pass the total revenue test, as the relatively lower price is charged to the more elastic segment of the market. (See Table 3.2.)

Table 3.2
Price Elasticity and the Impact of Pricing Decisions Revenue

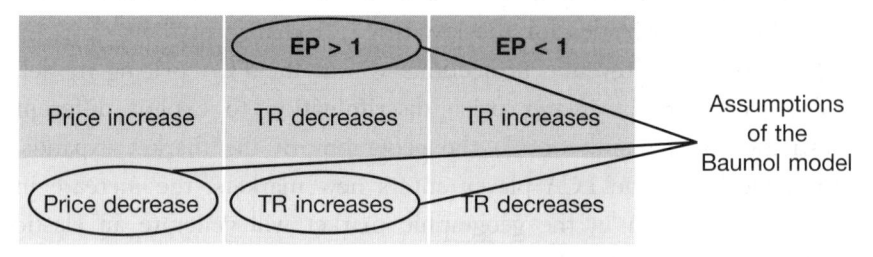

	EP > 1	EP < 1	
Price increase	TR decreases	TR increases	Assumptions of the Baumol model
Price decrease	TR increases	TR decreases	

Each of these pricing strategies allows management to price-position their products while taking cognizance of the boundaries of the trigger price. Price as a signal impacts on the magnitude of any price change and also guides as to the appropriateness of the price direction, for a given demand function. While recognising that demand can both shift and change in slope, the trigger price develops a strategic angle when complemented by the three price strategies just discussed. What is important is the relevance of elasticity to the debate; it is more than a response variable, and it has a very important and strategic role to play in any pricing game. While the behavioural models help to instill greater realism into economic modelling, the profit constraint is still an absolute. Should the firm continue to make extremely irrational decisions, then eventually the economic consequences of failing to maximise the profitability of the company will take their toll. The degree of leeway in performance would therefore be proportional to the size of the firm, its market share and the profit margins that it enjoys. Ultimately, it depends on management type.

Elasticity and the Want Paradox

If price is the key driver of revenues in the business model, then product price elasticity of demand has to be computed. Although net total revenue will increase for a product with elastic demand, as price falls there is a danger that in a product market wherein consumers expect more 'bells and whistles' net total revenue will fall as price falls. In other words, 'bells and whistles' reduce the price elasticity of demand. This has an interesting application to the low-cost airlines (LCA) pricing model. Low prices initially persuade passengers to switch from rail or ship to plane, but as passengers become more accustomed to airline travel, they expect more bells and whistles for the low price. A change in their elasticity will frustrate the revenue projections within the LCA pricing model, unless (1) there is greater price discrimination to exploit different elasticities of demand, or (2) the geography of the market expands. Paradoxically, as the LCA player enters new markets, the increase in player competition in the geographic market will generate an elastic (industry) demand. See Figure 3.3.

Figure 3.3
Pricing and Total Revenue Test

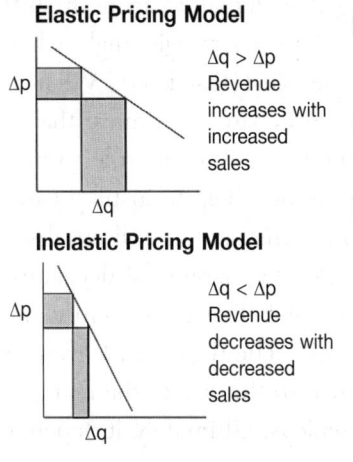

Elastic Pricing Model

Δp

$\Delta q > \Delta p$
Revenue increases with increased sales

Δq

Inelastic Pricing Model

Δp

$\Delta q < \Delta p$
Revenue decreases with decreased sales

Δq

- ☒ The elastic pricing model is applicable to emerging markets for mobile phones, retailing or LCAs.
- ☒ In contrast, the inelastic pricing model is more applicable to high-income markets or demand for product functionalities.
- ☒ The price range can change: elastic or inelastic depending on the market, product or service and on price as a signal.

	$\epsilon_p > 1$	$\epsilon_p < 1$
P ↑	Total Revenue ↓	Total Revenue ↑
P ↓	Total Revenue ↑	Total Revenue ↓

Significantly, passengers who may never have travelled by plane will be most vociferous in demanding the bells and whistles. It is the phenomenon of the want paradox: we do not need the product called 'unknown', but once it is available we all want 'unknown' and wonder how we survived without it. The fax machine, email and mobile phones are modern examples of this phenomenon, the impact of which is to reduce price elasticity. But product life cycle may be short, as new 'unknown' products emerge, displacing existing products – for example, email replacing fax – or more bells and whistles are expected, as with mobile phones, where preference is as likely to be determined by the pixel quality of the inbuilt camera, the speed of video download, gigabyte capacity for music content or some other functionality as it is by the actual price or tariff charged.

CHAPTER 4

Marris Hypothesis

> "Mark and learn, Amy.
> Mark and learn."
>
> **Charles Dickens**

Companies need to raise capital to develop new products and invest in research and development (R&D). The market value of a company is dependent on the underlying growth potential as measured by investment in product diversification. The Marris model offers an opportunity to chart a measure of profitability defined in terms of gross profit margin and capital turnover ratio. The measure can be captured by the equation $gd = gc = \alpha*p$, known as the balanced growth path (BGP) or valuation curve. One can observe guidance on profit margins filtering into profitability as an incumbent player competes against other incumbents and new entrants. Lower than forecast margins disappoint the market investors but also signal a degree of competition in the market. Financial markets adjust to every piece of information, and signalling quickly adjusts share prices to a fair value. Later in this chapter we explore how the BGP concept can be used to determine whether a company's share price at time period t is the best estimate of its true value. Part of the rationale for Framework $Tn=3$ is an attempt to find a pattern in observed behaviours and phenomena using management type and time as two key determinants.

However, the competition in the product market, which determines market share performance, can be defined in terms of $Tn=3$ under the umbrella of Edgeworth's (Chapter 1) strategic complements on price

– aggressive price matching – or in terms of strategic substitutes across the market shares. We address these issues later in this chapter. In the interim, suffice it to say that strategic substitutes may be captured by the zero-sum constraint, where a player gains market share at the expense of a competitor. The key point here is that if capital is raised to fund growth, for example, via product diversification, then the expectations of consumers regarding the product's bells and whistles will constrain the growth target if the product's technology lags behind the time-dependent preferences of the consumers. If a player can sell large volumes, it should help support the profit margin. Increased competition, for example, is a significant factor behind a decline in profit margin, particularly when the player is unable to differentiate fast enough in the market.

Our focus in this chapter is on the Marris model (1963 and 1966), whose 1966 formulation has become "the standard one for analysis of [the growth of] the managerially controlled firm" (Hay and Morris, 1991). In his model, Marris presented the hypothesis that managerial control would lead to growth as an objective, showing that shareholders were a less important constraint on such firms than financial markets. The Marris model is dynamic in the sense that it incorporates growth. Like Baumol's model, it assumes that management will act to maximise their utilities rather than profits, but in contrast to Baumol, it assumes that this will be achieved through growth rather than sales.

We have selected this model because it represents one of the few explicit analyses of firm growth and because it has a greater relevance today than ever before as management signal to maintain performance. More important, many companies today have too much cash on their books. Should they return cash to shareholders or investment? For example, both Apple Inc and Pfizer Inc have excess cash today, but do they have the investment potential in new products to secure long-term growth in time period $t+1$? By revisiting the mechanics of the Marris model 40 years later, we are able to present a signalling option that fits within the parameters of Framework $Tn=3$ and may offer management a cash cure. The simplifying assumption of a **balanced growth path** as the concave function in Figure 4.2 allows management to formulate a long-run equilibrium growth model in which the firm's rate of demand-side growth must balance its rate of supply-side growth, and in which explicit economic factors can be identified that influence both sides.

Dividends versus R&D Trade-off

Abstracting from the literature on the Marris model, there is a consensus that Marris proposed a model of key metrics of firm performance, including sales growth and profitability. Sales growth depends on the success of R&D expenditure in achieving product diversification. But management are faced with an interesting trade-off, as illustrated in Figure 4.1: to invest more in R&D or return cash to shareholder investors. We call this the dividends paradox. It is discussed in further detail on page 42.

Figure 4.1 shows that there is a trade-off between the proportion of profit paid out by the firm and how much it can grow – every time the firm reduces the dividend proportion by moving down the vertical axis, it can finance extra growth. The key issue for shareholders is whether or not the investment being financed by paying out less in current dividends eventually produces more profits and future dividends. Shareholders have to trust management on this.

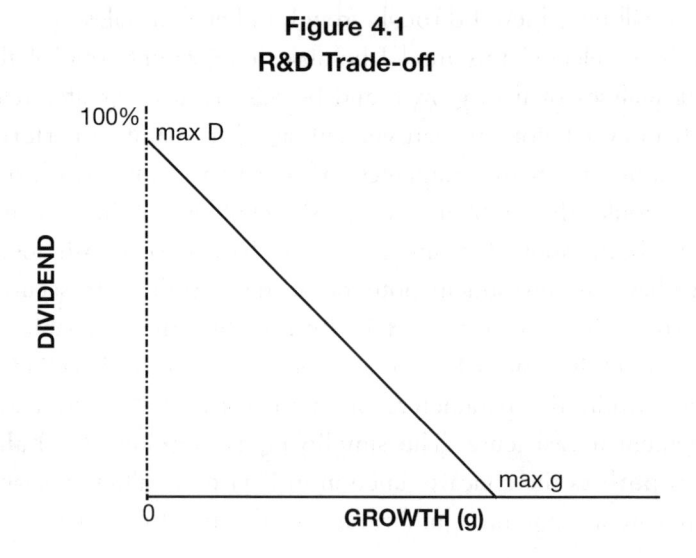

**Figure 4.1
R&D Trade-off**

The *gd* Equation

Where does a firm obtain its g_C supply of capital? Within the finance literature there are two sources, debt or equity. Contrary to the emerging theory at the time on the relevance of debt financing versus equity financing to the value of the company, Marris promoted minimal debt. Once equity capital has been injected into the company, it can be used for R&D expenditure and/or returning dividends to equity investors. So g_D, the demand for capital, has two sources, an internal management demand for more R&D expenditure and an external shareholder demand for more cash through dividends. There is a trade-off. The Marris trade-off can be summarised by the Koeller-Lechler equation:

$$g_D = g_C = \alpha * p$$

The equation uniquely determines the firm's equilibrium growth rate and the rate of return on its capital (p). According to standard accounting principles, the term p in Marris' model is influenced by the firm's capital (asset) turnover ratio, measured as output/capital. This ratio is an indicator of the operating effectiveness of the firm – the extent to which the firm's asset base has been used to generate sales. Relative ineffectiveness of the firm's sales efforts would result in a lower rate of return on capital, p, and a reduced growth rate.

Furthermore, the term p is also influenced by the profit margin on sales, measured as profit/output, which can be interpreted as an indicator of the firm's operating efficiency. We can rewrite the gd equation as follows:

$$\{\text{profit/output}\} \times \{\text{output/capital}\} = \{\text{profit/capital}\}$$
$$= \text{profitability} = p$$

Relative inefficiency of the firm's operations (expenses increase relative to sales) would result in a lower value for p. The presence of bounded rationality, for example, or the Penrose effect, though not specified as such by Marris, could result in inward shifts of the balanced growth path.

The firm's demand-side growth rate (g_D) is determined by the extent of product development. The extent of product development is then related to the firm's goal of increasing its profit rate. The achievement of this goal depends on the firm's managerial capacity to successfully promote product development. According to Marris, demand-side product development efforts should eventually lower the firm's rate of return on capital if one assumes diminishing returns to product development activities. Improvement of the firm's managerial capacity can be expected to moderate the demand-side trade-off between growth and profitability. The supply-side growth rate (g_C) of the firm's capital base is dependent on the extent of internal financing from profits, where the parameter α^* reflects the maximum extent of new investment that can be financed per unit of profitability. The value of α^* is determined by shareholders' interests in avoiding low profits and possible takeover.

The Dividends Paradox

Within the Marris model, management are faced with a trade-off between R&D expenditure and payment of dividends. Management do not wish to cease growing and so retain an increasing proportion of profits in time period t to finance increased growth in time period t+1. What happens when growth is curtailed? For example, this could arise in some product markets wherein the company is unable to differentiate quickly enough. To sustain the market value of the company, should management pay dividends or retain more modest profits? Scouller argues that management can enjoy fast growth while also benefiting shareholders; their retained cash is being spent better than if they invested it elsewhere. However, on account of management concern with their own security from takeover, they would be unlikely to push their activity so far as to dilute the market value of their own shares sufficiently to create a reverse risk of their own takeover. Eventually the new markets saturate, and unless other similarly profitable markets are found, the firm becomes mature and value peaks. However, within Framework Tn=3 dividends are regarded as signals and the payment of dividends can influence the share price. If the dividends signal is interpreted as lack of product innovation within the g_D side of the equation, then management have to engage in positive learning transfer (PLT) by communicating with shareholders that in time period t+1 value will be restored. The share value to one investor may signal the company's ability to pay dividends, but the payment of dividends signals to another investor an absence of R&D and innovation. Therefore PLT is one way to ensure that share prices reflect the execution of strategy.

Marris Balanced Growth Path

In Figure 4.2, rather than at a point x where the profit rate would be maximised, management choose to situate the firm at a point y where, under certain constraints, the growth rate is maximised. Marris represented his classic trade-off outcome by plotting the profit rate p versus the growth rate g. Alternatively, in Figure 4.2, we have plotted the firm's 'valuation ratio' – the name given by Marris to the ratio of market value to underlying asset value, subsequently named q by Tobin – and growth rate. It allows for an interesting trade-off: management may

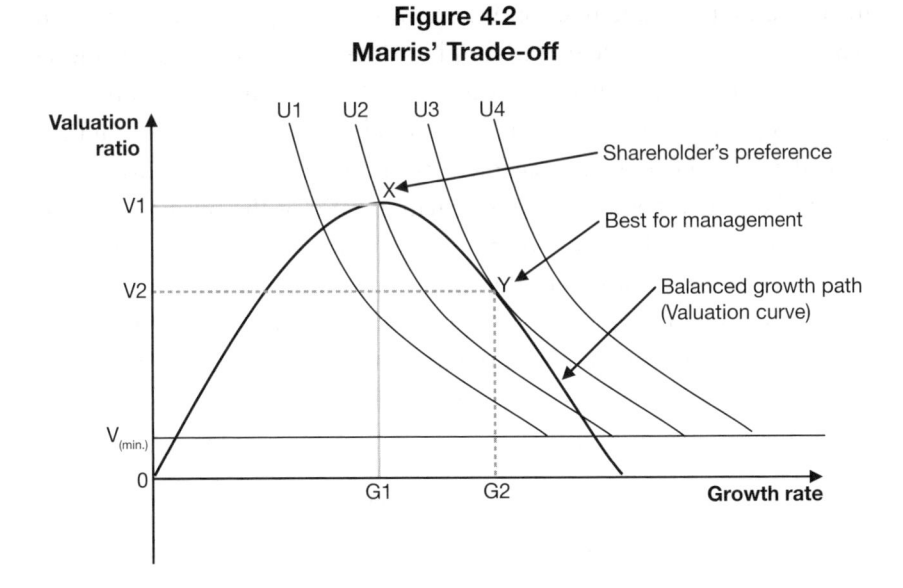

**Figure 4.2
Marris' Trade-off**

pursue a faster growth rate at the price of reducing the valuation ratio to below its maximum. Note that a robust empirical relationship between low valuation ratio and statistically observed probability of takeover was identified by Bartley and Boardman in 1986.

The Marris model is also of interest because it focuses on the vulnerability of a firm. The valuation ratio V is used to identify the best growth rate that is acceptable to both the shareholders and management. U1 to U4 are management indifference curves. They represent the third or Z variable. In the classic Marris model, the third variable is managerial satisfaction or utility. U4 provides the highest utility to management. However, because it is beyond the balanced growth path (BGP), it is unachievable. Moving to the left to U3 generates a tangency point v on U3, which is tangent to the BGP. It provides the highest possible utility to management. However, point x on U2 provides the best return to shareholders because of a higher valuation ratio. In choosing between these two points, management have a bias to set G2 as their ultimate organisational objective.

Quasi-Marris Model 21st Century

In his original model, Marris advocated that corporate growth could be manipulated to maintain an optimum dividend-to-profit retention ratio that keeps the shareholders satisfied but does not retain too high a level of profit, creating a cash-rich business ripe for a takeover. This implies a degree of control on share value that would seem difficult to sustain for even the most effective management team. There are simply too many other factors that could affect the valuation ratio of the business beyond corporate growth. Deciding on how best to achieve growth becomes a crucial issue for management during the life cycle of a firm.

For example, if management wish to grow by product diversification there is a constraint inherent in the Marris model, the gd equation, that is fairly acute for firms that opt to grow through product diversification rather than by acquisition:

$$gd = f.(d, k)$$
$$\text{growth} = f.(\text{retained profits})$$

where d is the dividend rate as a signal and the parameter k represents the percentage of successful new products. The k parameter ultimately depends on R&D, advertising and promotion; and the spend on these variables depends on the profits, which ultimately depends on the efficiency of the firm.

A Marris type would seek to achieve organic growth through product diversification by investing more in R&D and paying lesser dividends to shareholders. There will be a trade-off between these two variables, and therefore, we have defined the X variable to be the R&D expenditure and the Y variable to be dividend. The third variable is the valuation as measured by

$$\text{Marris v} = \text{market value/asset value} = \text{Tobin's q}$$

As asset value (net book value) grows with R&D investment in gd and more shareholders invest in the company on the strength of the PLT, the v increases and performance as measured by profitability increases from levels P1 to P3 in Figure 4.3.

At point X, the neoclassical equilibrium, is the profit maximisation point for the company with the maximum dividend, D1, paid out to shareholders. This can be achieved by investing R1 in R&D. The profit

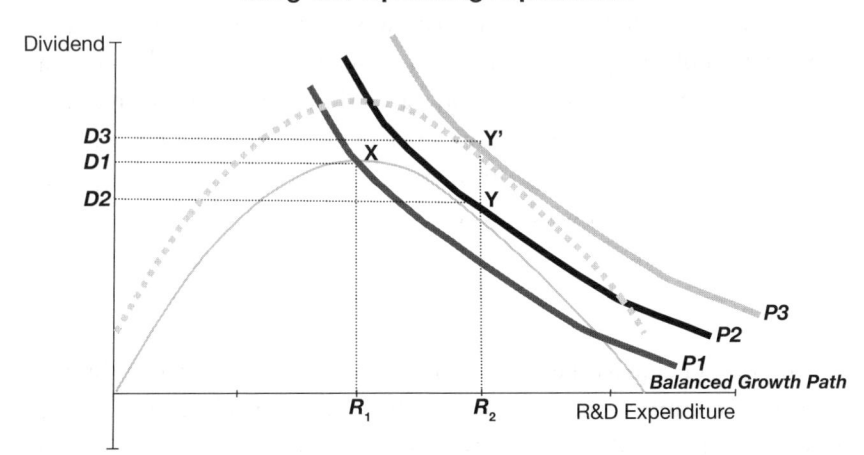

Figure 4.3
Long-run Operating Equilibrium

line (indifference line) for this position is reflected in the P1 curve. A Marris type believes that in order for a company to be able to sustain into the future it is necessary for it to grow and create value. As such, management would invest in its R&D, assets and technology at the expense of short-term profits. By reducing the dividends from D1 to D2, and increasing the R&D expenditure from R1 to R2, it will attain a new equilibrium at point Y. The objective over time through these infrastructural investments is to grow the company such that its performance will also increase from P2 to P3, with the balanced growth path shifting upwards, attaining a new dynamic equilibrium at point Y.

The Marris v

The Marris v is an important variable. It is not unrelated to Tobin's q. If $q = v < 1$, then the assets are not fully utilised in the company and it would be a good investment to buy shares when $v < 1$. The buying of shares would increase the share price and the market value in time period $t+1$. There are many financial performance ratios, such as the Hamada equations, Sharpe ratio, Jensen alpha, Traynor ratio and Sortino ratio, in addition to α and β of the capital asset pricing model. They represent a measure of financial elasticity by measuring financial performance. The Marris v does likewise, measuring the elasticity of asset value to market value but defined in terms of management type to ensure that growth (gd) determines value (v). The Marris security parameter, a, is a combination of a range of key financial indicators (KFIs), such as leverage ratio, liquidity ratio and retention ratio. Fundamentally, management are secure if the firm carries minimal debt, delays dividends in time period t in favour of R&D in time period $t+1$, and engages in positive learning transfer to reassure investors.

Agency Costs

There is a benchmark rule in Framework $Tn=3$: the higher the valuation of a company, the less likely is the threat of takeover. This rule, however, intimates that dividends should stay high to maintain the share price. Alternatively, management may wish to invest more profits to secure more growth with a risk that the value of the company falls. If the higher valuation were perceived by shareholders to be at a maximum, then shareholders would prefer that higher valuation, so it behoves management to persuade shareholders that the risk of a fall in value can be captured by a higher growth rate. Management inability to persuade shareholders gives rise to agency costs. The agency costs arise because of the separation of the ownership and control of a firm. Berle and Means, who published a classic study in the 1930s, argue that this separation affords management a considerable degree of discretion; the trust between shareholder (as principal) and management (as agent) comes under threat if management abuse the discretion, and the financial loss to the principal is called an agency cost. One way to tackle the agency costs is for management to design a trust mechanism between shareholder and management, thus enabling shareholders to entrust money to management with a reasonable expectation of getting something back.

Marris Type Positive Learning Transfer

A central theme in designing trust is the context of the management decision, that is, how the decision is observed by shareholders. Shareholders may adopt a Bayesian-type rule, seeing what they want to see about management and the firm. Management should resist this. How? They could signal a positive learning transfer to shareholders whereby management with prior experience in (games with) value-growth issues introduce positive expectations of a stronger performance (higher value for the firm).

This could be achieved through persuading shareholders to view the decision as a continuum rather than as a dichotomy. In other words, the decision has to be framed as a decision about more growth and higher value rather than less value and more growth. Shareholders can then observe the decision of management as a chance wherein making a gain in circumstances where they trust management outweighs the risk of making a loss.

In terms of the competition, management should evolve as strategic players in the sense that they understand that their actions are likely to lead to a reaction from competitors. In other words, they become conscious of the fact that the price of their product depends on the decisions of their competitors, affecting both capacity and market reach of the product. For some products, the combination of overcapacity and technology standardisation will drive prices down, creating low profit margins. In these circumstances, management as a player engage in patching by re-mapping portions of the product's business to changing market opportunities.

If higher value is sacrificed for higher growth in the interim, one element of the trust mechanism should be that the product becomes **a brand with global reach**, dominating its market through expenditure on R&D and advertising. This combination of decisions is what we define as the diversification acreage. Within the acreage of diversified products, if a product is not achieving its global reach and is underperforming, then management should spin off the product.

Marris Type

By the 1970s, Mueller had advanced the Marris model by advocating a life cycle of firm growth. Mueller's life cycle was a major qualification of the classic linear characterisation of the growth path of a firm advocated by Marris. Borrowing the arguments first identified by Mueller, we can also think of the Marris model as follows: first, sustainable long-term growth requires market growth; this can be achieved, at a cost, by R&D. In turn, new markets must be supported by new productive capacity. The combined costs of bounded rationality, agency costs, R&D and new capacity may be called the costs of growth. They require cash flow. Cash flow may be obtained from retained profits, new share issues and new debt.

The amount of the last, in any given period, is constrained on one hand by the unwillingness of lenders to offer unrestricted sums relative to the firm's existing scale and size, and on the other by management's fear of the risks, to them, of excessive leverage. Management can pursue a growth rate (implying specific costs of growth and profit retention ratio) that would maximise the firm's valuation or q-ratio. Alternatively, management may pursue a faster growth rate at the price of reducing

Table 4.1
Return/Risk for *gd*

	High Growth/*gd*	Low Growth/*gd*
Return	Growth drives value	Value drives growth
	Less dividend signals	More dividend signals
Risk	Inability to differentiate fast enough	Innovating at the speed of the slowest firm

the valuation ratio to below its maximum. If management have growth-preference, the model closes, with a unique management desired growth rate, and thus the factors that encourage managerial behaviour encourage faster growth of firms; for example, more expenditure on R&D and marketing and hence a **positive learning transfer** between management and investor shareholders.

It is the trade-off between dividends in time period t and more growth in time period t+1 that gives us our first glimpse of this particular Marris type of management who are motivated by achieving sustainable long-term growth. Management are necessarily risk-averse, working out a risk profile for all decisions in terms of likely outcomes. Ultimately the decisions are binary: either product x or y, but not x and y. The choice of product x carries with it the opportunity costs, in terms of lost revenues and market shares, of not selecting product y. But provided the costs are minimised, the contribution of product x to the achievement of sustainable long-term growth in the company will be positive.

Understanding type will help in identifying the trade-off facing a rival competitor, and this understanding may enable management to predict the likely reactions of the competitor, a significant factor in any competitive interdependent market structure. But in order to understand management behaviour as observed, we need to know more about management type. The third variable is key, and there are three possible candidates: (1) utility from the classic Marris model, (2) the valuation ratio from Framework Tn=3 and (3) profitability.

The latter was applied to Apple Inc as an exercise in MBA workshops and is illustrated in Figure 4.4, while estimation of the Diageo plc BGP can be found in McNutt (2008).

If the motives of management reveal their type, then a Marris type, for example, may now be summarised as follows: sustainable long-term growth requires market growth; this can be achieved, at a cost, by R&D. In turn, new markets must be supported by new productive capacity. We are advancing an equation to compute the BGP.

McNutt's BGP equation: $y = a(x - h)^2 + k$.

Figure 4.4
Balanced Growth Path for Apple Inc

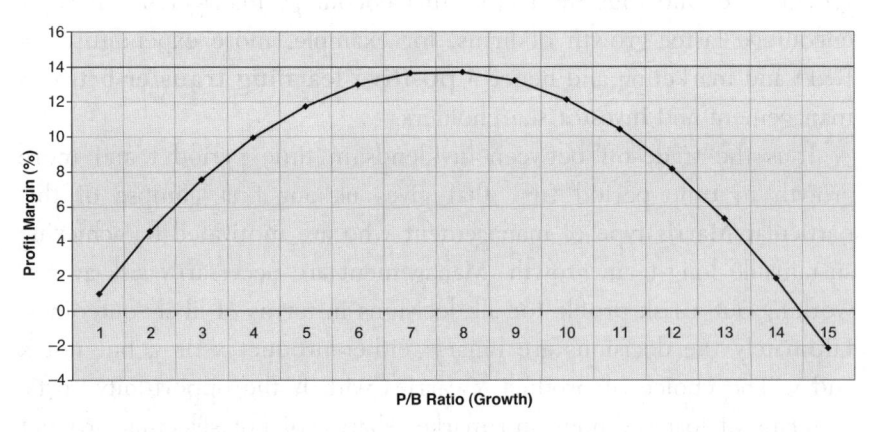

Table 4.2
Marris' Third Variable

Variable X	Variable X	Variable Y	Third Variable, Z
Classic Marris	*gd*	V	Utility
Diageo plc case in McNutt (2008)	*gd*	Share price	V
Apple Inc in this chapter, Figure 4.4	Price/Book ratio	Profit margin	Profitability

The equilibrium position of the BGP in time period t+1 can expand or contract, as illustrated in Figure 4.3. The costs of growth in t+1 can be explained by the combined costs of the Penrose effect, the costs of R&D and new capacity. They require a cash flow.

A cash flow may be obtained from retained profits, new share issues and new debt. If the company does not borrow externally, then the only source of finance for achieving growth is retentions. Herein lies what we shall refer to as a Marris trade-off: **more** in R&D requires more cash and may mean **less** to shareholders in the form of dividend payout. Growth is therefore a function of retained profit.

Marris Signalling

The Z-variable equation represents that unique third variable that signals management type. In the case of a Baumol type, the third variable is sales revenues, and the trade-off facing management is that time period t will include profit as one of the (X,Y) variables. In the Marris type, we have advocated value v, the market capitalisation of the company divided by its asset (new book) value as the Z variable. Management of Marris type will signal value maximisation through *gd* growth maximisation as the key variable. Signals can be read from listening to CEO interviews; and as equity traders and analysts become more sophisticated in analysing volatility in equity markets, management may become less concerned about reaching the third variable level and more concerned about signalling their intent to do so. During periods of great movement in equity price, analyst predictions and management signals will feed off each other so that for the share price, p, a signalling maximum could be reached at:

$$\text{Signalling maximum: } (\sqrt{p})/p^{-1}$$

For example, a share of number 9 (£9 or €9) could reach a signalling maximum of 27. The author is examining the significance, if any, of this number. Most analysts are bullish on companies with a price/earnings ratio in the range 8 to 10 and a dividend yield of 5 per cent. Equity becomes an attractive investment with relatively lower price/earnings ratios. The numbers send a signal. A signalling maximum recognises the fact that a signal is already in the price. For example, companies with expensive shares that then have a profit downgrade as analysts' targets are not met in time period t may not necessarily experience a fall in the price of shares as investors await target announcements in time period t+1. A good stock to buy is one that is well-placed to weather the storm of mis-signalling as analysts lag behind as chief executive officers engage in PLT. In the classic Marris model, there is mention of a security parameter, a, and it may be possible to rewrite that Marris security parameter in terms of the capitalised value as determined by the signalling share price maximum:

a = signalling maximum valuation/replacement cost of net assets

This would allow us to assemble the three ratios, Marris v, Tobin's q and the Marris security parameter, as a measure of stock market value. If we were to exclude financial stocks and exclude intangible assets such as brand value or intellectual property rights from the computation of the replacement costs, then a value such that a = v = q < 1 might indicate a 'buy'.

CHAPTER 5

Cost Technology

> "Feel the force, Luke:
> let go of your conscious self and act on instinct."
>
> ***Star Wars***

Competition has changed: there was once a reliance on price and quantity, the two classic firm-specific variables; now it is quality and innovation, which are quintessentially firm non-specific, yet the consumer benefits directly from them. One key parameter is the level of consumer demand for the product. In a zero-sum world, for example, one firm could be challenged to meet extra demand due to falling sales of the rival. Whatever the reason for the extra demand, management strives to set the production rate equal to the rate of consumer demand. This just-in-time approach can result in waste elimination and lead time reduction. Historically, batch production has been considered optimal due to long machine changeover times and the requirement for immediate satisfaction of customer demand. This can involve high stock holding costs for the firm. Production smoothing is the process of adapting the production rate to variations in customer demand. From management's perspective, a high-quality product is still delivered to market on time, with significantly reduced costs.

The production technology within a company has been presented in neoclassical models as the constraint imposed on achieving optimal firm size. In the management models there is no optimal size, but rather the growth of the company depends on the abilities and capabilities of management. If the management are not performing, the company fails in its objectives. Bounded rationality is one reason advanced to explain management underperformance. In this chapter, we advance the idea that management are faced with a capacity constraint that they do not fully understand. The reason for this is failure to further understand the cost technology embedded in the production.

There is a greater need to improve the lines of communication between the production, procurement and sales divisions within a company, whether it be manufacturing or service oriented, otherwise management will be faced with a production–demand dilemma. One way to overcome this dilemma and obtain a sustainable cost advantage as a cost leader (CL) is to understand the cost technology. The cost technology has been broken down into five constituent steps in this chapter, so that management can decide at time period t which step applies to their company. The steps can be followed in sequence and may take up to seven years to complete. In the case of Canon, illustrated by Figure 5.1, the process took ten years over a period that saw the emergence of Canon as a formidable CL-type player in the market for copiers, scanners, printers and cameras with a sustainable cost advantage in its market.

Figure 5.1
Canon and Cost Leadership Type

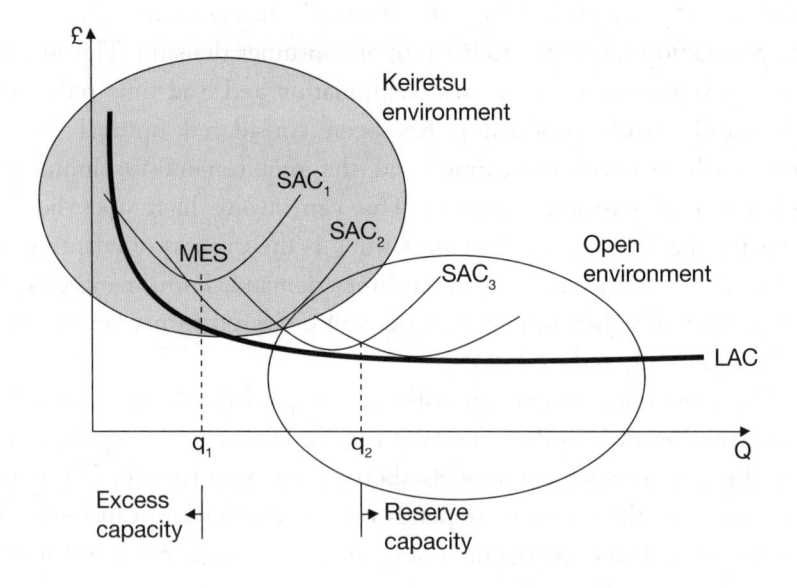

Production–Demand Dilemma

For management, understanding capacity is key to ensuring cost efficiency throughout the production process. Framework $Tn=3$ focuses on the link between the cost and product curves and also distinguishes between excess capacity and reserve capacity. In obtaining cost efficiencies, management must be prepared to allow production to determine demand. Why? If demand determines production in a product market with innovation and increasing product differentiation, there is a risk that sales will lag as consumers opt to purchase the latest innovative product. A company with lagging sales will carry inventory and risk carrying obsolete products in a market with ever-changing consumer preferences. Therefore, in the 21st century many companies risk carrying excess capacity as they are unable to sell what they have produced, simply because consumers no longer prefer their products. This becomes more acute in those markets where innovation, technology and product differentiation are key drivers of demand. One way to escape this dilemma is to engineer the production process so that production determines demand.

Against that background, we introduce the cost leadership model with the five strategic steps that act as a filter, helping to identify the cost leadership (CL) type of player. In achieving this status in its industry, management would have to ensure that a number of steps are followed within the company. We adopt the premise that the companies are not single-plant, single-product manufacturers serving only a national market. This may be the case for a small engineering plant, but in the aggregate, cost leadership is obtained in multi-plant, multi-product companies that transcend national or indeed regional market boundaries.

Collectively the five steps define the production relationship within a firm. Step 1 is to distinguish between economies of scale and economies of size. Size should be interpreted as a global economy of scale that can be achieved only once management neutralise the zero-sum constraint. Step 2 focuses on maximising the average productivity of labour, realising that the measure of average productivity is the inverse of the average variable cost of production. Step 3 requires the introduction of a normalised wage system within the company, offering incentives to the workforce so that a reduction in the number of employees is carefully matched with an increase in productivity.

Step 4 is key; it is about controlling costs: once costs are controlled or fixed during the production cycle, management can focus on decreasing the average fixed cost. This can be achieved by hedging raw materials required during the production cycle, offering workers a fixed term or fixed term-fixed wage contract or by outsourcing or by rebalancing costs back to the suppliers in the supply chain. Finally, step 5 requires management to identify the capacity constraints within the company and to clearly demarcate excess capacity from reserve capacity at each plant within the production technology. Reserve capacity requires the building of additional capacity in the plant in the expectation of demand; excess capacity is to be avoided – it can arise if the company is unable to differentiate its products fast enough in an ever-changing consumer market. The ideal outcome is one of zero excess capacity, with a reserve capacity in production.

Wage Normalisation

From the geometry of the product and cost curves, we can observe an inverse relationship as follows:

$$AVC = w/AP_L$$

From this equation, we note that the average variable cost (AVC) is inversely related to a measure of average productivity (AP_L), depending on the wage level, w. It is a simple observation but one that can be easily overlooked by management. The management at TooBig plc have decided that 7,000 employees is too big a number to sustain as they search for cost efficiencies. So they decide to downsize to 4,000 employees, with a plan to lay off 3,000 employees. This is achieved usually with generous redundancy payments.

In many cases, the most productive take the package on offer; after a period of time, management at Smaller plc with 4,000 employees realise that they are not achieving their cost reduction objectives. In fact, costs have increased in real terms at Smaller plc. One reason is that the 4,000 employees remaining are not as productive on average as the 7,000 were. The 7,000 employees included the 3,000 most productive workers who took the redundancy package and ended up being re-employed by Smaller plc on a fixed-fee contract. In other words, costs are increasing at Smaller plc because productivity has fallen. This is not the only explanation for increasing costs, but it is often a contributor.

It would have been more judicious for TooBig plc to focus on the productivity issue, encourage the most productive staff by way of incentives, and encourage the least productive to leave the plant. It is important to note that average productivity can increase if existing workers are more productive so that $q^* > q$ for a given number of workers, L, hence $q^*/L > q/L$, and productivity has increased because output has increased to q^*. This is contrary to a more conventional approach that reduces the number of workers from L to L^* believing that $q/L^* > q/L$: sadly, this result may not occur. Productivity falls as the level of output, q, does not increase, and q will not increase if the most productive workers exit. Management should remember that the total product of L produced on a fixed amount of K is the same as the average product of K when L is fixed. If we assume that when K is fixed, its value is 1, and when L is fixed, its value is also 1, then the following relationship holds:

$$AP_L = TP_K, \text{ when } K = 1$$

With a normalised wage structure there is a greater focus on productivity, as the wage structure offers incentives to the most productive workers to stay and the least productive to exit. There could be share options, for example, and a range of productivity incentive contracts present in the plant. A normalised wage sets $w = 1$, and we have

$$AVC = 1/AP_L$$

So, notwithstanding how costs are reduced, sustainable cost advantage can be obtained only if there is an increase in productivity as a consequence of the cost-reduction measures.

Excess versus Reserve Capacity

During the production phase it is important for management to understand the capacity constraints facing a modern production facility. We distinguish between excess capacity and reserve capacity. For each plant size there is a minimum efficient scale of operation (MES). At this point average costs are at a minimum, and production beyond this point will give rise to diseconomies of scale and rising costs. However, production is often at a production level to the left of the MES plant size. Traditionally, this is the point of excess capacity, and the older arguments were developed in economics accusing the monopolist of producing with excess capacity. Why bother to produce more (towards the MES output) when there was no other rival supplier in monopolist's market?

However, modern firms today, and not in a monopoly position, can be producing with excess capacity simply because they are faced with an ever-increasing demand for their product at a time when they are unable to product-differentiate fast enough to meet the demand. Technically, they have spare capacity in the plant, which translates into excess capacity with a slack demand for the firm's product. Unless the firm is able to differentiate its product in the market, it will be producing at a point to the left of its MES, with excess capacity. This is equivalent to **capacite**

**Figure 5.2
Theoretical Short-run Cost Curve**

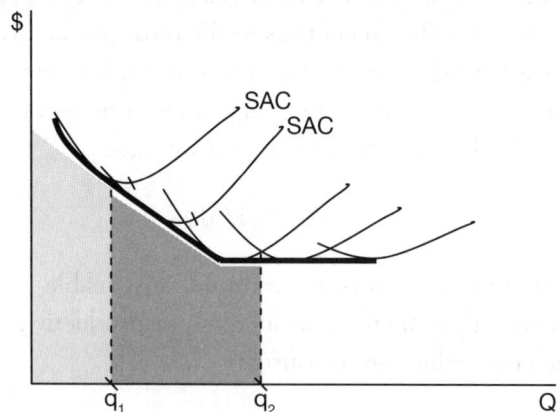

Cost Technology

excedentaire. This is not a preferred position – for management to be located to the left of the MES – because it is simply not cost-efficient.

Conversely, reserve capacity arises when production is at a point of LMC = 0. It is best to think of reserve capacity as **installed capacity** used by management when it is required. In other words, different levels of production can be reached at zero marginal cost. This is because the company has built in additional capacity into the production process early on in the production cycle. This situation could exist in a product market where **production determines demand**: this is very relevant for the management of innovative products such as mobile phones, printers and video game consoles.

Reserve capacity is illustrated with an L-shaped cost structure for the LAC. In economics we refer to this as level of production, as production where constant returns to scale prevail. However, more interesting is the case where L-shape neither increases upward (looking like an elongated U-shape) nor trends downward (representing a declining LAC). In this

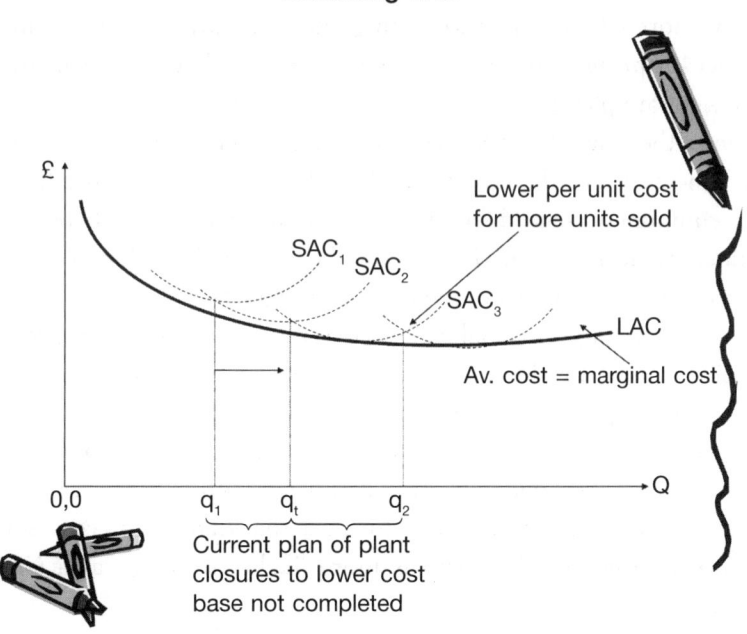

Figure 5.3
Declining LAC

£

SAC$_1$ SAC$_2$

SAC$_3$

Lower per unit cost for more units sold

LAC

Av. cost = marginal cost

→ Q

0,0 q_1 q_t q_2

Current plan of plant closures to lower cost base not completed case the cost structure implies that output is not large enough to observe whether or not average costs will rise. Management may prefer to be cautious and not push production too far in case costs increase.

Cost Leader Type

The demand (for a product) may be so demanding – what we call **reserve capacity on demand**, or CoD – that it is better for the manufacturer to allow production to control demand. This is contrary to the conventional wisdom that it is demand that drives production. Arguably, it may be more cost-efficient to engineer a plant with reserve capacity so that production determines demand.

Functionalities are precisely what the consumers are demanding. For example, a printer is a printer + copier + scanner + fax machine. Or a mobile phone is a telephone + MP3 player + mega-pixel camera + email communications device. The combination of different functionalities $(q_1, q_2, \ldots q_n)$ generates **economies of scope** at step 1, such that

$$C(q_1, q_2) < C(q_1) + C(q_2)$$

It is more cost-efficient for management to have one large plant that produces a printer and a copier and a printer + copier than to have three separate plants.

Once the plant has reached its size, then economies of scope can be engineered into the cost technology. But it may take time. If so, the time component should be signalled to the market. If there are any production delays, then they should be signalled as shipment delays, not as a failure to meet demand. The signal is necessary in order to calm investors while allowing management to plan for additional capacity at the production plant(s). Consequently, management are in a stronger position to control costs. What one observes is a flat-bottomed cost curve; and with seasonality in demand or a new innovative product on demand, the company with reserve capacity in production will be better placed to meet that demand at cost-efficient levels of production. The firm is more likely to emerge as a CL type in its market.

Checklist: Five-Step Analysis

Step 1: Distinguish between Economies of **Scale**, Economies of **Size** and Economies of **Scope** within the production process.

Scale: $\Delta K = \Delta L = 2\%$ and $\Delta q > 2\%$

Size: Achievable in competitive market $\Delta q = 4\%$ in phase 1; decide ex-post in phase 2 of the production process the most optimal, ΔK or ΔL; and implement in phase 3.

Scope: Across production so that $C(q_1,q_2) < C(q_1) + C(q_2)$

Step 2: Focus on increasing average productivity of labour AP_L. How?

Note that $AP_L = w/AVC$, where w = wage proxy and AVC = average variable costs.

Step 3: Normalise the wage structure: let $w = 1$. In other words, offer the workers incentives or bonus payments as productivity increases, revisit the organisational structure and consider the production process as a nexus of contracts.

Step 4: Control more of the production costs to allow more costs to come under control during the production process. Hedge positions on material inputs, minimise exchange rate risks, and have workers on fixed-wage, fixed-term contracts with incentives per flexible manufacturing.

Step 5: Demarcate between excess capacity (idle capacity) and reserve capacity (installed capacity), bearing in mind that excess capacity can occur if the product is not sufficiently differentiated fast enough in the market to capture market sales. At the point of production in phase 1, ensure sufficient installed capacity to meet demand in later phases of production.

A key assumption here is that management can change the plant size. This can occur due to economies of scale from the larger-size plant when to the left of the minimum point on the LAC curve. The minimum point on the LAC is the **optimum scale of plant**, the MES. SAC represents the cost structure of the smaller-scale plant, and the corresponding minimum point on the SAC is the **optimum rate of output**. The challenge for management is to move from optimum rate of output to optimum scale of plant. Division and specialisation of labour can bring about the economies of scale; likewise, the adoption of advanced technology, for example, robotics and computer technology, can trigger economies of scale.

Management today seek to obtain economies of scale in the supply chain by outsourcing to a lower-wage economy, as with the move from the European Union to the economies of Brazil, Russia, India and China in equipment manufacture, textiles and back-office financial administration. However, with outsourcing, management must ensure that productivity does not decrease at the outsourced plants: simply offering lower wages does reduce the variable costs, but average costs will decline only if productivity is increased. As output increases, management are faced with a second challenge in understanding the capacity constraints that may emerge during the production process. Arguably, management intent on cost leadership will not produce at the minimum point on an SAC curve because if they did, they would lose in the sense that they could produce at a still lower average cost, with a slightly larger but underutilised plant if it were to the left of the minimum point of the LAC, and with a slightly smaller but over-utilised plant if it were to the right of the low point of the LAC curve. This is McNutt's dilemma: do management build a larger plant that may be underutilised or retain existing plant that may be over-utilised? The dilemma cannot be solved unless management introduce a normalised wage structure and demarcate the point at which present production levels are in terms of capacity. The economic argument is simply that the cost curve derives its shape because of five CL-type steps.

De Nihilo Nihil Fit

Rational management know the old adage that 'nothing comes from nothing' so a decision has to be taken. For example, Brand Inc in time period t could signal the launch of a new product in time period t+1 and allow a 'word of mouth' moon-shot to exist in the market. So consumers who want to purchase the product in time period t find that it is not available. Demand is not determining the production. It is by signalling that Brand Inc is able to create a **ghost demand** in time period t so that the production cycle in t+1 can be engineered to meet that level of demand. However, it is the production at time period t+1 that determines the demand at t+1.

This back-scatter approach to production would be characteristic of a CL type at step 5. The risk in delaying production is the loss of a first mover advantage (FMA) in a product with a growing demand for its functionalities. However, the gain in observing another player succumbing to demand, as a product underperforms due to lagging consumer expectations, is the second mover advantage (SMA). In the production game there are two conjoint decisions:

> FMA loss < SMA gain
>
> FMA gain > SMA loss

CL type is not about an obsession with cost cutting per se, ensuring that every purchase no matter how small is logged into a central accounting system. CL type is about mistake-proofing against these two decisions. Mistake-proofing can be assisted by a regret matrix (Chapter 10), which computes the opportunity cost or loss of deviating from an optimal decision.

CHAPTER 6

Players and Vertical Blending

> "You tremble, carcass,
> but you would tremble still more
> if you knew where I am going to take you."
>
> *Marechal de Turenne*

Blending is the coexistence of two types of game play, one affirmed by signals (management type) and the other displayed in effective action (player type). For example, the appointment of a new CEO will introduce a new type of management, so we need to further understand how the type of management is blended into the type of player. Vertical blending occurs when the type of management influences the type of player. Management type is embedded within the firm and signalled to the market as a player type. This is important because it links the performance of the company to the type of management. Management are appointed by shareholders or private equity because of their type. Some are known as ruthless cost cutters, some believe in growth by acquisition, some believe in organic growth. The appointment of a new CEO sends a signal to the market, and it is for the market – competitors and equity analysts – to identify the management type in order to avoid misreading of signals.

Weak vertical blending occurs when the culture of the firm or company, composed of all its stakeholders, may influence the type of management by getting management to do what they do not want to do by influencing or shaping or determining their actions. Stakeholders may prefer to persuade management as to a course of action, coerce management to take an action, that is, to secure their compliance by controlling their thoughts and actions. Rational management as a player may simply duplicate the reasoning process of the stakeholders. However, taking control is an irreducible fact because taking control emanates from the control of information within the organisation per se and through the game process. As the game unfolds, management's actions ultimately define the type of player the company has become in the game. Vertical blending is an exercise of type rather than a case of structural determination. This assumes that it is in the **exerciser's or exercisers' power** to act differently (Lukes, 1975).

Signalling

Once management realise that they have the power to act differently, and act differently, blending is complete. Therefore, the process arises when management's actions mean something to them as individuals – in other words, they are capable of processing their own experience in a manner that can confound all predictions by a near rival, all predictions based on the fact finder's observations or the near rival's description of the type of management. The difficulty for management is trying to understand the blend in a rival firm, and the difficulty in coping with the blend may be due to the fact that the type of management per se has been formed, during the game, in reaction to competitors.

The key issue is to provide a template for how management can best represent the blend created within the company in actions or words. To do that is to understand the words and actions of management: the signals. The template is based on player interdependence in a game. While the actions are interdependent, for example, in a sequential pricing game of leader-follower, the signals by which they are prompted are mutually independent. This is because player actions mean something to management as individuals, and different managements will interpret the same signal differently. Consequently, we refer to taking an action as the observed reality: the game success or pay-off, the Porterian competitive advantage, is obtained from knowing when and how to act.

The Core of Vertical Blending

The type of player arises from an economic foundation based on a theory of oligopoly. Oligopoly is a market structure characterised by a few players, usually fewer than five. The number is significant because with so few players there is a greater interdependency amongst the players, and a greater probability that one of the players will recognise this and try to exploit it. The object is to maximise the economic position of the player, the pay-off, and indeed to obtain a preferred outcome for all players, that is, the market.

In oligopoly markets we are more likely to observe a consolidation across the market shares of the players in time period $t+1$. We make this assumption for the purposes of this book. Consolidation is at the point at which the zero-sum constraint becomes acute. A fact finder will observe constant market shares. Player A's market share loss from 35.2 per cent to 35 per cent translates into a gain for player B. For game theory to become an appropriate tool of analysis, we require that the underlying environment does not change too fast, so that we can equate management behaviour in terms of an equilibrating behaviour. In other words, player A realises that the range 35 per cent to 35.2 per cent is the best market share obtainable given the likely reaction to their action from other players as competitors in the market-as-a-game. So player A does nothing to regain the lost 0.2 per cent market share because there is a probability of losing 0.2 per cent. Once player A realises this outcome, we are at a Nash equilibrium, and the realisation may be due to the fact that one of the players may have played a game in an earlier time period.

Strategy

Player A decides to reduce price, and the key is whether or not B will react to any price movement. If A believes that B will react, then it is imperative for A to have a reply to the likely reaction from B. Hence we have the strategy triangle of action-reaction-reply. If A does not have a Nash reply, then it is because A did not expect a reaction. The key to understanding our definition of strategy in Framework $Tn=3$ is to ask: Why did A not expect a reaction? What is it about B's pattern of behaviour that led A to believe that B would not react to any price change from A? One of the contributory factors is B's type, defined in terms of the type of player and the type of management. Type of management refers to the subjective behaviour of management in terms of a preference for pricing or organic growth. Type of player is to be understood in terms of the patterns of observed behaviour of the company in the market. For example, we seldom observe price wars between Pepsi and Coca-Cola in their core market, unlike with Sony, Nintendo and Sega, who experienced a lengthy price war in the video games market in the 1990s. A key question is: Given their strategy, how should they behave? For example, player A reduces price to correct declining total revenue, but competitor B does not know the reason why the observed price has fallen. Could player A be a Baumol type? If so, the price move observed is a one-shot move and may not require a reaction from player B. So, to avoid any misunderstanding, player A could reveal its type as a Baumol type. It helps to understand some basic economics of strategy in order to identify a type of management.

Limit Pricing Model

Otherwise known as the Bain-Modigliani model, the limit pricing model defines a game between an incumbent type and a camouflaged entrant type. In order to understand player type, we will work with the Bain-Modigliani or limit pricing model.

The limit pricing model (see Figure 6.3) represents the classic example where a player considering entry into a new market is presented as a demonstration of non-cooperative game theory. The biggest uncertainty faced by the new entrant is predicting the reaction of the incumbent player in the market, whose perceived options are to either be accommodating and allow entry or to react aggressively with price cuts or discounts. An aggressive response could reduce the value of the market due to an ensuing price war. In this analogy, the incumbent is more likely to cede market share to avoid a price war. If the decision is taken not to enter the market, the pay-off for the new entrant will be 0 and the incumbent retains the full value of the game (10). Should the company decide to enter, the incumbent has two strategies to pursue: retaliate with aggressive price cuts, thereby risking a price war that will leave it with a reduced pay-off of 2, or accommodate. In the above example, the new entrant cannot afford such a price war and will fail to return a profit from the venture (losing 7). If the incumbent accommodates the new entrant, its pay-off is reduced to 8 through ceding market share to the newcomer, who makes a successful entry with a profit of 5. Self-interest (profit maximisation) governs the likely response of the market incumbent, thereby negating the value of any probability calculation if the incumbent's first response is to prevent entry. While it is sufficient to analyse the probability of the reaction options, it is necessary to be guided by what actions the rational, self-interested respondent is likely to reply with in the game.

Retaliation

The reply will depend on the player's belief about the type of player the competitor is in a game. Like the Galton's ox weight contest, each player will observe how individual errors and biases in predicting likely reactions will tend to cancel each other out as the sought-after information about type is distilled in some aggregate measure of belief. Players will either adopt a binary approach or not:

Player A asks:

Binary: Will player B react? Yes or No
Non-binary: Player B will react: Probability = X%

Notice that in Figure 6.1 each of the options open to the rival results in a change in the total value of the game. Retaliation would lead to a price war in which lower profits would devalue the total returns available to all players. In this example, the resulting market losses are 5. Alternatively, allowing the new company to enter would grow the market value overall to 13, the sum of the pay-offs 5 and 8. The strategies open to the players are clear. Notice that the first decision lies with the new entrant, and the subsequent response by the incumbent makes this a sequential game. Outlining the strategies forms the key to systematic thinking about which one of those strategies is the optimal path to follow.

Limit Pricing Strategy Set

Do not enter, do not retaliate (status quo)
Enter and retaliate
Enter and accommodate

**Figure 6.1
Market Entry Decision: Extensive Form**

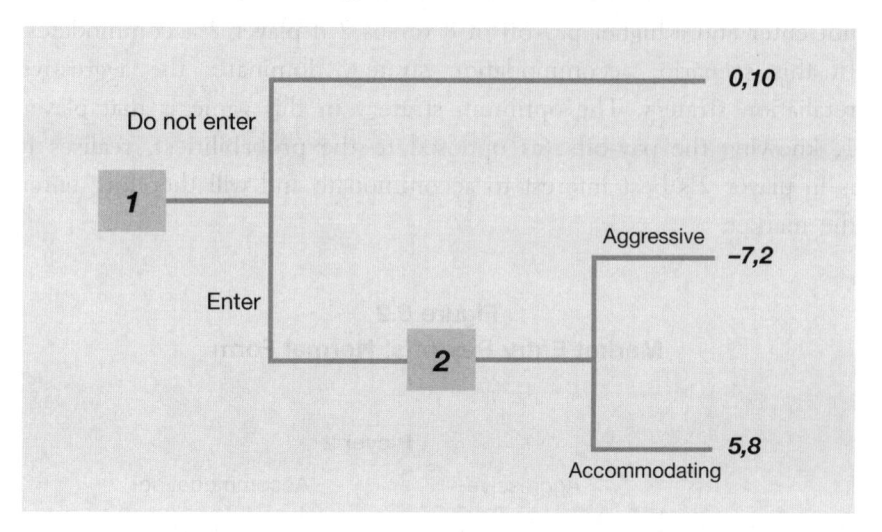

```
                                              0,10
      Do not enter
   ┌─┐
   │1│
   └─┘
                              Aggressive
                                              -7,2
      Enter
                         ┌─┐
                         │2│
                         └─┘
                                              5,8
                             Accommodating
```

Dominant Strategy

The same game can be represented in pay-off matrix form as illustrated in Figure 6.2. The game matrix directs the players to only logical strategic choice. Player 1 assumes that player 2 will act in rational self-interest, and it is in player 2's interest to assume the reciprocal arrangement applies. Suppose that there is a first strategy that 'under no circumstances yields a lower pay-off and sometimes does better' than a second option. It is said that the first strategy **dominates** the second.

In Figure 6.2, player 1 has no dominant strategy. If they do not enter they will have no pay-offs, and the incumbent does not need to react and will retain the market value. The 'do not enter' strategy only dominates the 'enter' strategy if the incumbent reacts with discounts. A zero pay-off is better than a loss of 7.

However, for player 1, the 'accommodating' strategy of the incumbent would result in a higher pay-off for the new entrant than not entering at all. It is clear that player 1 has no dominant strategy. Player 2, however, has a clear dominant strategy. In both cases of 'do not enter' and 'enter', the incumbent is better off accommodating the new entrant. This is indicated by the pay-off of 10 if the newcomer does not enter and a higher pay-off of 8 versus 2 if player 2 accommodates. In this scenario, accommodation strategy dominates the aggressive retaliation strategy. The optimum strategy in this game is that player 1, knowing the pay-offs (as opposed to the probabilities), realises it is in player 2's best interest to accommodate and will therefore enter the market.

Figure 6.2
Market Entry Pay-offs: Normal Form

		Player 2	
		Aggressive	Accommodating
Player 1	Do not enter	0,10	0,10
	Enter	–7,2	5,8

Player Types and Signals

Markets characterised by incumbent management who regard a threat of entry as an actual plan of entry at a time period yet to be decided can be described as contestable. A contestable market is as close as we get to the textbook competition. However, as geography begins to define the market boundaries, incumbents face the possibility of a de novo entrant type. A **de novo type** is a player in the same geographic market as the incumbent in at least two product markets that are complementary to a third product market, the incumbent's market. The de novo type will seek to gain the synergy and acquire the incumbent. So a de novo entrant type grows by acquisition as the boundaries of the market expand. The boundaries can expand due to technology, innovation or change in regulations. With changes in technology at time period t, a player can exit a game and return in time period t+1. Netscape, for example, exited the Internet browser war with Microsoft but has re-entered the market-as-a-game as Mozilla and is competing with incumbent players Microsoft and Apple Safari. This is a good example of a **newborn** player, who re-enters the game as technology changes. Kodak could be defined as a newborn in that having allowed the digital revolution in cameras to pass it by, as a newborn player it has adopted digital technology.

The difficulty for an incumbent is to determine whether or not the entrant type is a **potential entrant type** with no intention to enter in time period t, or a de novo type, who has every intention to enter. Depending on the management's belief, actions will differ as to how best to limit entry. Each action will further act as a signal to the other players in the market and may invite a reaction from the other incumbent players. For example, if an incumbent type believes with a high probability that entry will happen, the incumbent reduces its pre-entry price, triggering a reaction from the incumbent players who have lost a price differentiation advantage as a direct consequence of the pre-entry price reduction.

Believable Bills

In markets, the incumbent type is easily recognised as an endogenous historic player already in the market because of, say, government imprimatur or national geography or a survivor in the market-as-a-game. A defining characteristic of an incumbent type is protection of market share, and this requires effort and management time to attempt to delay or prevent entry by an entrant type. Vertical blending with such players creates 'believable Bills' based on the belief that if entrants enter the market, then profits post-entry would be driven to zero. The believable Bills will do everything to delay, retard or prevent entry. Accommodation is not a dominant strategy for believable Bill type (see Table 6.1).

Entrant types, by definition, are seeking entry, but they can be subdivided into potential entrant types, who threaten to enter at a point in time, and de novo entrant types, who actually do enter at a point in time. The difficulty for an incumbent type at a point in time is in determining the type of entrant, and the incumbent management's belief as to the entrant's type of management will determine the pre-entry actions of the incumbent player.

**Table 6.1
Player Types**

	Incumbent Action Believable Bill	Probability of Entry Doubting Thomas
Potential Entrant Type	Reduce price Increase output	High & incorrect Low & correct
De Novo Entrant Type	Dividends policy Increase share price	High & incorrect Low & correct

Doubting Thomas

The entrant type will signal to the incumbent type its intention to enter the incumbent's market. This gives rise to the 'doubting Thomas' incumbent who does not perceive a threat of entry at a point in time. The doubting Thomas knows how the entrant will act because he knows the entrant management will act rationally. However, the entrant is a player, and if the entrant's signals are deviant, the doubting Thomas may not be able to respond should the entrant actually enter the market.

If the believable Bill incumbent believes that the entrant type will actually enter the market, then the incumbent management will take actions to deter entry, for example, they may reduce the market price or increase the quantity produced in the pre-entry period.

However, if the entrant type is a potential entrant type with no intention to enter in time period t, then the believable Bill incumbent has reacted to a threat of entry that will not materialise at time period t. If an incumbent management behave in such a manner, then they believe that the threat of entry was credible, that is, that there was a high probability that the entrant type would have entered, hence the rationale for reducing the market price. Conversely, a doubting Thomas incumbent would not have reduced the price on a threat of entry but at the higher price may have left itself exposed to price differentiation by other players, including other incumbent players who may opt to exploit the price differences.

Rank and Type

If all the incumbents have the same belief structure, the low price will signal to the entrant that the incumbent expects entry in time period t and that the incumbent believes that the entrant is a de novo type. That means that there is a probability of entry at time period t. Earlier we had distinguished between believable Bill and doubting Thomas: the bB reaction is to prevent entry whereas the dT reaction is to dismiss the threat at this point in time. Conversely, if the incumbent player initiates a signalling game by an aggressive dividends policy, this may be interpreted as a signal of the presence of a de novo entrant in the expanding geographic market. In other words, a bB player, concerned about a possible threat of takeover, may opt to return capital to its shareholders in the form of generous dividends. This would occur if bB management were Marris type.

However, if a second incumbent feels threatened by the price action of the first incumbent, then there is every possibility that both incumbent players could end up in a price war. The players that survive a price war are referred to as **extant** types. A price war outcome may have been the original intention of the entrant type who had earlier signalled its intention to enter the incumbent's market. But the price war outcome arises simply because one incumbent reduces price in the belief that the entrant is a potential entrant type and likely to enter at time period $t+1$.

Conversely, in the case of a de novo entry, for example, one incumbent may place a takeover bid for a second incumbent player, either as a defensive strategy (two incumbents are less likely to be acquired than one alone) or by breaking rank. The presumption with rank is that incumbents in a given national geography have not or do not intend to acquire each other until an external shock to their market. The shock may manifest itself as the arrival of new technology, the adoption of new innovation or the emergence of a de novo entrant in the newly expanding geographic market. But one player may have anticipated the external shock and readjusted its decision making to reveal its type as an endogenous player only in the post-shock environment. To consider this further, we need to understand the decision making within the blended type, that is, we need to define and comment later on the decision quantum, DQ. There is additional external pressure on the firm today that is removed from the concerns of competitors – the interpretation of the decision per se by the fact finder in a national competition agency. Lieberler, Easterbrook and Sidak have suggested that what passes for antitrust policy has been simply an attempt to force firms to act myopically.

An incumbent type, for example, can readjust its actions from any agreed rank; an incumbent that breaks rank is referred to as an **endogenous rival** type. The presumption here is that the players in a rank game are able to act jointly because each player observes the behaviour of the others, and that the customers obey the rules: think of a taxi rank, where the rule is that the taxi at the head of the queue goes first and a random customer arriving at the rank is requested to join the queue for a taxi. The rank is a good example of rational cooperation that is both desirable from the customer's point of view and sustainable from the player's point of view. A rank is more acceptable than a cartel because altruistic motives are ascribed to the players, and thus the players can act jointly in the knowledge that their joint behaviour will not be condemned by a third party.

In order to understand the behaviour of an endogenous rival type we need to consider the significance of ascribing altruistic motives to the players. For example, at one time it was regarded as in the public interest to have a national monopoly with responsibility for, say, public utilities, a view that has progressed into a national champion theory and probable xenophobia. National banks have traditionally served a national population; with the transcending of national boundaries in a single European market, the same national banks begin to rethink their strategy. Either they become the target of de novo entrants as they expand beyond national geographic boundaries or they break rank by acquiring smaller incumbents or adopting new technology faster than other incumbents, signalling an aggressive organic growth strategy that remained silent under the rules of the rank. However, because we use banks as a fictitious example, and bank behaviour is not immune from antitrust investigation, banks as players would be advised to deny a rank ever existed, notwithstanding the observations of the fact finder.

Why Enter? Entry Function and Technology

It may be helpful for management to derive an entry function in order to re-focus the debate on the restrictions on entry:

$$E(q) = q^{2m}$$

where $q = [Q - q^*]$, Q is total demand and q^* is incumbent output, or q_1 in Figure 6.3. Of particular interest is the exponent term '2m' – it will generate the concavity of the entry function. The specification of the entry function and its concavity highlight the restrictive nature of entry. $E(q)$ translates into an actual market share if entry was impeded. As the incumbents increase q^*, q tends to 0 and $E(0) = 0$. The function $E = E(q)$ maps the optimal level of exclusion output for each number of entrants. Technology and economies of scale in production make exclusion output easier to produce – this could be interpreted as a fall in the price of exclusion resources. This would imply a higher return on each dollar spent on exclusion and a shift upward in the function. The equilibrium outcome is one of a smaller number of smaller firms than before entry deterrence.

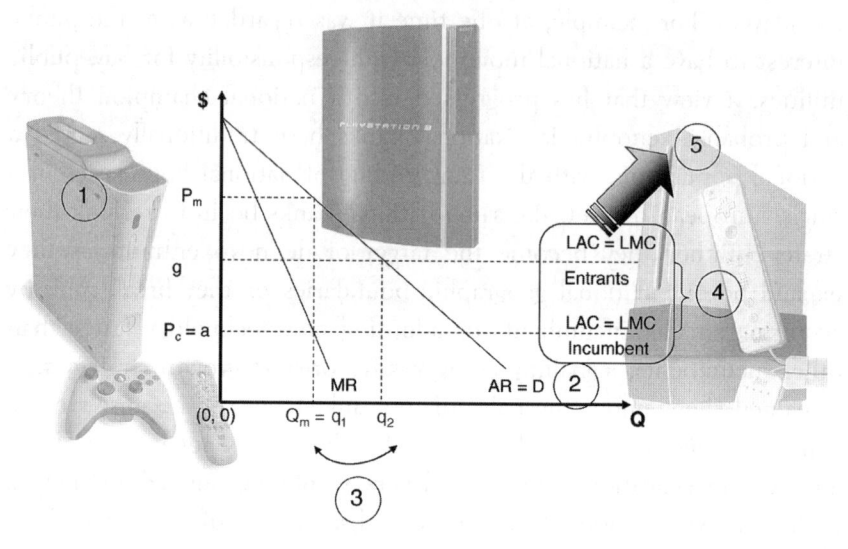

Figure 6.3
The Bain-Modigliani Model (Limit Pricing)

An unanticipated change in technology may have left incumbent players with considerable excess capacity even though demand has not expanded. Alternatively, as Landes and Posner argued, a decline in demand may have left firms with excess capacity. Whatever the reason for excess capacity, suppose the dominant player is matched with an entrant with the capacity to produce another X per cent of output without a significant increase in marginal cost. In this case, the excess capacity of the entrant would limit the dominant incumbent's efforts to raise price above marginal cost. Competition policy might argue that the incumbent's excess capacity may make any threat by an incumbent to engage in predatory pricing – to keep out new entrants – more credible. If the incumbent monopolist has used real resources in order to deter entry, the issue to explain how the opportunity cost of those resources factors into the traditional costs of playing a game. New entrants probably would not find an industry operating at excess capacity an attractive one to enter even in the absence of predatory threats. The E(q) function would support this type of outcome, an outcome that requires a debate on credible mechanisms and the Bertrand dilemma, which is discussed in Chapter 9.

CHAPTER 7

Dark Strategy

> "Your words are like the handiwork of my ancestor Daedalus; and if I were the sayer or propounder of them, you might say that this comes of my being his relation and that this is the reason why my arguments walk away and won't remain fixed where they are placed."
>
> **Socrates**

Competitors know of each other's existence. The zero-sum constraint is acute. In this context, type is not only about conduct and behaviour; it is also about making decisions, carrying them through and taking action. We may regard the courses of action open to management as strategies of the firm. A strategy is one firm's plan of action adopted in the light of management beliefs about the reactions of its competitors. In this scenario, for example, a firm's pricing policy per se may not affect the shareholder value; it will, however, affect the shareholder value through the management's reaction to the action of a competitor to the original pricing policy.

In other words, management must understand that action leads to a reaction that further requires a reply. Every action must have a (Nash) reply. This hypothesis is maintained throughout the book. It simply means that management should not be surprised by events in time period $t+1$ that emanate from their action in time period t. As with our opening example in Chapter 1 on the possible launch of a gPhone ahead of the launch of an iPhone, the signal on the possibility of a gPhone in the market-as-a-game is called a moon-shot. A moon-shot is a signal that players deny, but if one player believes the moon-shot to be credible then they are observed as acting sooner than the cost technology or capacity may have facilitated at time period t. It is worth pointing out that the gPhone was launched only in September 2008. But was the iPhone released too soon, in the summer of 2007?

Answers to this type of question fall into the unknown of strategic behaviour, what we refer to as **dark strategy**. Will Nokia enter the laptop market? Will Dell enter the smartphone market? These are challenging questions as at September 2009, answers to which could, in part, be accommodated within Framework $Tn=3$. By observing type, by understanding the convergence of technologies, players would be in a better position to consider the market that they should be in at time period $t+1$.

Mistake-proofing

The issue of launching 'too soon' depends on the inherent cost technology of the player to ensure that they do not have capacity constraints on the launch of the product. But a greater risk, in the absence of a Nash reply, is that competitors can secure a **second mover advantage** by emulating the original players' functionalities. Nokia, for example, is in a strong position to secure a second mover advantage in the evolving smartphone market. By differentiating between music content with xPress models, focusing on the more professional users with N-series and E-series phones, and focusing on time period $t+2$ with mobile Internet, Nokia can secure that competitive advantage provided Apple Inc are not surprised.

Player strategy is when management realise that they are in a game. In economics, rational man makes optimal choices guided by well-defined and stable preferences. There are preferences on costs – marginal cost pricing, ABC costing and incremental costs. Management are faced with a **supply correspondence dilemma**: on one hand there are competitors squared off against cyclical consumer preferences, the Penrose effect squared off against internal x-inefficiencies and costs squared off against price positioning. There will be capacity constraints in what is traditionally referred to as the short-run problem coupled with planning horizon issues in the long run. Making a decision has to translate into taking an action. It is not easy. For example, planned obsolescence, productivity and niche batch production characterise the production technology of many firms. Endogenous rivals whose type may be unknown at a given time period may emerge, and the Nash premise becomes more acute – the essence of modern competition.

Belief System

For management there are tensions between economic routine and argument and the desire to follow one's own instinct in business matters. The company may have a smaller asset base but be generating greater pre-tax profits; hence it is making more profit from the same level of assets as its near-rival, and this will be reflected in the stock market as the company's being observed to outperform its near-rival. It is important for management to learn the lesson that the best player in terms of profitability and performance measures is not necessarily the biggest player in the market. And the biggest player is not necessarily the best. The belief system is captured by the conjectural variation [CV] in the following way. If player A has a $CV = 0$, then they do not expect a reaction from a competitor; conversely, with a non-zero CV a player does expect a reaction to their action in a game.

It is this that distinguishes between knowing that a decision has to be made and knowing when and how to make that decision. Knowing that a decision has to be made is referred to as making a decision; knowing when and how a decision has to be made is referred to as taking an action. The latter term is analogous to making a move as understood in game theory, that is, the players make their moves when they actually decide on the strategy to be adopted. In brief, a strategy is a string of moves or actions.

Therefore, management's subjectivity is an essential property; it refers to management's sense of past, present and future, which makes management at once a creature of history. Simon (1958) and the behavioural approach have argued that management are bounded rational in decision making, while Penrose (1958) has argued that management are limited in their abilities. Both subscribe to a view that management are exposed daily to complex information, reliant on subordinates to inform them of the precise usefulness of pieces of information. Nonetheless, management must take the first step in decision making. In taking the first step they can apply their knowledge as management guided by 'laws' of individual behaviour and linked to other rival management by the game and to internal management by the organisational structure of the company. It is this coalescing of the links reminiscent of Poincare's 'collision of ideas' that yields something new in a company and a degree of unpredictability for observers of patterns of behaviour. Simple ideas generate more complex ideas, and simple actions generate more complex actions, through a process of vertical blending, whereby the type of management blends with the type of player.

Behaving Strategically

From first principles we could define the economics of strategy as a combination of the Penrose effect (PE) and the Nash premise (NP). The latter simply requires a player to have a reply function, anticipating the likely reaction from the player's action. In their pursuit of growth, for example, management come to realise that a growth rate implies specific costs of growth and trade-offs. In Mueller's (1972) life cycle interpretation of firm growth, desired growth is often limited by both internal and external constraints. Internally, there are Penrose limitations on the ability of management to achieve growth, and this is coupled with external constraints in a zero-sum market where growth of the firm slows down. Management do not wish this to happen.

Costs are committed to maximising growth, and management insecurity about the impact of the zero-sum constraint could push their motives so far as to dilute the market value of the company sufficiently to create a reverse risk of takeover. Understanding the type of management of the competitor becomes crucial in this story. Once management take cognizance of a rival competitor's interdependence, management have become a player in a game and decisions are said to be strategic. Management behave strategically when they come to understand that each and every decision is followed by an action that is observed by the market participants. This gives us a definition of the strategy equation:

Strategy Equation
S = PE + NP

It is a combination of minimising the Penrose effect and ensuring one has a response to any reaction to one's initial decision in a game. The Penrose effect can be minimised by understanding type, and with a non-zero conjectural variation the player has anticipated a reaction. Ideally, we as third party observers – the fact finders – would like to understand how the decision was achieved and, for each alternative in the decision-making process, to understand why it was rejected, and by whom. In other words, we need to understand the context of the decision-making behaviour. The management of competitors would like to know this as well, but particularly they would need to understand the history of the actions for each of the market participants in the decision-making process. The play of a firm consists of a detailed description of the firm's activities in carrying out its move. This is discussed in Chapter 9 through the reaction functions. If A and B were to move to a price war, for example, their play would be a description of their actions, but the intriguing question is how they made the decision to engage in a price war.

It is by knowing when and how to make a decision for each player that a description may be forthcoming. But rivals will do everything to keep one another guessing. Interpreting management as participants in a game is nothing new. However, in this book we have approached management as participants from a different angle by introducing the significance of type in understanding management behaviour and company strategy in product and service markets, in local, national and global markets. The focus on type is a key driver to understanding actual, observable behaviour. The behaviour translates into a conflict of subjective outcomes in a non-cooperative market wherein management as individuals compete against each other for market share; however, they keep each other guessing on the next action.

Decision Quantum

The blending of management type and player type creates a decision quantum (DQ), that is, the individual or group of individuals that make decisions or take action or both. The blending of management type and player type is supported by the property of conjectural variation (CV). The earliest models of oligopolistic behaviour assumed that firms formed expectations about the reactions (or variations) of other firms, called conjectural variations. The Cournot, Bertrand and Stackelberg models can be interpreted as conjectural variation types (see Table 7.1). The quantum is composed of management type and firm, as they morph into one game-playing entity, the player. If a player per se finds itself in a market with fewer than five competitors, it behoves management to identify each rival as a type of player. At its simplest, all players are incumbents in the smallest bounded market and any new player wishing to enter that market is an entrant type. Post-entry, the entrant type evolves into an incumbent type and the blending of management type with entrant-turned-incumbent player type begins to unfold. The player is an extant (still existing) type. This becomes more acute in a market where the number of players is less than five, where interdependence, the quintessence of oligopoly, is a key driver of competitor reaction. For example, both Sony and Nintendo are extant players in the video games market, Sega is not, and Microsoft morphed from an entrant type in 2000 to an incumbent type today.

If DQ1 has a CV = 0, then DQ1 does not expect any reaction from DQ2; conversely, if DQ1 has a CV ≠ 0, then DQ1 anticipates a reaction

Table 7.1
Game Theory Types

	CV = 0 Expect No Reaction Surprise	CV ≠ 0 Expect Reaction No Surprise
Price Variable Price signals	Bertrand type	Stackelberg type
Non-price Variable R&D expenditure, advertising	Cournot type	Chamberlin-Porterian type

from DQ2 and formulates a reply strategy (see Table 7.2). The reason why a reaction is anticipated may be due to the management's reading of the signals from the type of management blended within the player type that has become DQ2. For example, if DQ2 was characterised by DQ1 as an extant player, then there is less likelihood that DQ2 would follow a price reduction by DQ1 than if DQ2 were characterised as an entrant type.

Table 7.2
Reply Strategy

	Type of Management	Signal
CV = 0	Bounded rational Penrose effect	Not in a game No reply strategy
CV $\neq$ 0	Player	Reply strategy in a game

Our treatment here is concerned with management acting only as DQs rather than as individuals, each DQ attempting to predict the actions of other DQs but not cooperating explicitly with them. This really is about management team interaction. It assumes no cooperation, but the outcome may sometimes be interpreted as implicit cooperation between the DQs. Take the example of DQ1 reducing price with a CV $\neq$ 0; DQ2 follows with CV $\neq$ 0, and DQ1 replies in what appears to a fact finder as a sequencing of price tumbles.

Players will either adopt a binary approach or not. In the Marris type, there is an inherent threat of takeover, and it is this threat that influences management to take action, for example, to engage in share buy-back or payment of generous dividends. There is empirical evidence to support the view that share price movements are correlated with dividend payments. Competitors would observe and may infer a Marris-type strategy based on an aggressive dividend policy within the company. An aggressive dividend policy carries with it the opportunity cost of funds not spent on more R&D, as well as lower growth for the company and the possibility of reduced future dividends. The business model works until the company is no longer on a balanced growth path, that is, unable to differentiate products or to innovate due to lack of funds at a time when the share price is increasing in the expectation of a change to the business model.

It is useful to address the issue of risk as understood from the premise that management are risk-averse but that being risk-averse does not preclude the taking of risks. In the context of game strategy there is a burden of loss in the interpretation of strategy in the context of actually playing the game with rival management. Otherwise, the interpretation of risk falls back on the issue of whether it is judicious for management to play the game. Indeed, it may be the case that management do opt not to play or that the understanding of type is wholly inappropriate for some managements and their respective firms. The latter could define management who, in effect, increase volume in order to maximise sales revenue, cut prices and largely ignore the presence of other firms. It may be a Baumol type.

The management philosophy known as *kaizen* has captured the attention of management over the past 30 years. It is a generic term incorporating numerous management techniques with a promise of increased productivity coupled with a reduction in inventories, errors and lead times with radical realignment of the production technology. Described by Imai (1986) as "the basic philosophical underpinning for the best in Japanese management", *kaizen* has emerged as a process-oriented, customer-driven strategy for corporate success (1986). It has given management the capability to quickly adopt and adapt their manufacturing processes to changing customer and market requirements. Management terms such as TQM, JIT, *kamban* and the 5-S programme are process-oriented concepts.

Poka-yoke

There is a lesser-known term that goes to the heart of our discussion of type and strategy: known as mistake-proofing or 'poka-yoke', it is adaptable as a concept to understand management type and risk (see Table 7.3). Management by nature are risk-averse, but being risk-averse, does not preclude the taking of risks. Indeed, the risk, however quantified, has an opportunity cost of real resources, and the management team has to balance that cost with the possible gains. Gains from, say, launching a new product, exciting an episodic price war or relocating a plant may be forthcoming. The risk element is to be interpreted in terms of management as a player finally adopting a contingency plan to complement whatever motive is driving their action. The strategy adopted is observed by competitors as an action. So, for example, whether or not to launch a new product is a binary choice: launch the product or do not launch the product, in the latter case parking its launch until later. Either way, the competitor can interpret the action and draw inferences about the type of management. If the expected return for not launching the product, $E(r_A)$, is greater than the expected return for launching the product, $E(r_B)$, management take the risk and delay the product launch at this juncture.

To understand this, we need to realise that the $E(r_A)$ is computed as the nth-root of the different risks as perceived by the player. If a player decides not to launch a product, the opportunity cost of lost revenue, for example, is a risk r_1 that has to be balanced against the opportunity cost of resources devoted to producing a product that might fail, r_2, resources that could be used elsewhere within the firm, r_3, or indeed in R&D expenditure on a different type of product, r_4. But one additional factor in computing that risk is the likely reaction from a competitor. If a player, for example, adopts a strategy, call it strategy 1 (S_1), then we would ordinarily associate a risk, r_1, with that strategy play. However,

Table 7.3
Poka-yoke

	Make a Decision	**Take an Action**
Knowing that	No error in the game No surprise signal	Poka-yoke Moon-shot is credible
Knowing how Knowing when	Poka-yoke Lost first mover advantage	No error in the game No surprise Nash reply

in order to integrate poka-yoke into that strategy, we would have to associate a row vector of risks, **R**, such that $R = (r_1, r_2, \ldots r_n)$; and for each r_i there is an expected return $E(r_i)$, so that management as a player adopting a poka-yoke position in trying to ensure mistake-proofing compute the nth-root of $\sqrt{\{E(r_1) + E(r_2) + E(r_3) + \ldots + E(r_n)\}}$. The action that is S_1 is contingent on r_1 with an nth-root expected return. Across the strategy set, **S**, there are S_1 to S_n, and the strategy with the maximum return as computed with the nth-root formula is the adopted strategy. The choice is binary, that is, management as a player will choose strategies from a set of strategies and can refer back to historic $E(r)$ for any related strategy.

Burden of Loss Standard

The complexity of the strategy set mirrors the complexity of playing the game; there is a **burden of loss** standard that impinges on management in adopting mistake-proofing or 'poka-yoke'. In other words, the burden of loss standard requires management to minimise the firm's exposure to loss. In many respects the interpretation of strategy is in the context of actually playing the game with rival management, while the interpretation of risk falls back on the issue of whether it is judicious for management to play the game. Making a decision, and knowing that a decision has to be made, are crucial. As noted, it may be the case that management decide not to play a game per se but proceed with business. Whether this happens or not depends on management type, technology and time. In a world where management can influence rivals' actions by their type, a reliance on profit maximisation or shareholder value as the key driver of management behaviour may no longer seem reasonable. Making a decision, and knowing that a decision has to be made, is crucial.

Management in oligopoly markets find themselves coming closer to the rhythm and pattern of real price movements. Prices are no longer arbitrarily guided by a march towards the Holy Grail of a perfectly competitive price. Rather, prices fall into a pattern that pervades the market for products, and management have to redeem themselves through their behaviour in the firm. Management's rational nature can help management decide to accept the reality or to change the pattern of observed behaviour through their own actions and reactions in the market. The economic price standards appear arbitrary or are imposed by institutions without any reference to the right reason or the preferences of management. There are price opposites of the perfectly competitive equilibrium, for example a cartel-like price, which can be turned into a negative signal (quaternity) when included with monopoly and dominant positions. So in this view, the business world management, robbed of their rationality, must avoid a cartel price or monopoly position because otherwise their behaviour will be constrained and retarded by external factors.

Strategy Set

A fact finder may observe play in a market by observing management actions, but for management the situation is more complex. Observed behaviour may not be repeated, or, as in our fictitious example, player A may not have expected a reaction from B because in the past B did not react. This is a crucial point in understanding the relevance of management type to a meaningful and pragmatic definition of strategy. Management make decisions every day. Many of these decisions are internal organisational-type decisions to do with budgeting, personnel or finance. The how and when of those decisions, the taking of actions, are generally confined within the organisation.

If we return to our fictitious example, player A may not have expected a reaction from B because in the past B did not react, so A observed a pattern of behaviour and did not have a reply. The converse is equally important: Why did B react? What was it about B that required it to divert from past behaviour? We will look at a few explanations in terms of type of management, zero-sum constraint, market systems, market share consolidation and innovation (see Table 7.4). Each will provide a template to overhang the strategy set.

The nub of the issue is this: when the taking of an action spills over into the market, it inevitably leads to a reaction from a rival. The identity of the rival may be unknown, or indeed the reaction of a particular rival unexpected. Not every day do management necessarily take an action

Table 7.4
Blended Management

Type of Player A Is Determined by:	Firm A = Player A	Firm A ≠ Player A
Zero-sum interdependence	Yes	No
Market system	Yes	No
Market consolidation	Yes n < 5	No n > 5
Innovation and time	Yes	Yes
Type of management	Vertical blending	No blending

that triggers a likely reaction from a near-rival in a market. Equally, not every day do they necessarily take an action that requires knowledge of likely reactions from near-rivals in a competitive market. Taking an action to do nothing at this juncture translates into the making of no decision and may be observed as such by the near-rival.

Today, for the majority of companies, the management team has to evaluate the risks associated with market participation. They can indeed integrate and adopt mistake-proofing or a 'poka-yoke' into their decision making: management evaluate the risks, decide to play the game and become players, and thus proceed to adopt strategies accordingly.

The important element in all of this is that management are risk-averse, implying that they evaluate the risks, take the risk with the greatest expected return and enter the market as strategic players. Non-participation, or admission that strategic behaviour is inapplicable to one's firm, is, in and of itself, a strategic decision, whether the management wish to concede that point or not to the other market rival participants. It is the nature of the market-as-a-game that another firm will interpret that decision strategically – it may signal, for example, old traditional management styles, it may suggest a possibility of poaching market share, it may signal a lack of R&D expenditures or whatever. But the management who opt not to participate have to take some responsibility for that decision should it inevitably leave the firm exposed to the vagaries of strategic game play, playing catch-up in a rapidly changing business world. This would be close to the concept of short-termism and could probably best characterise a type traditionally referred to as 'risk-averse management'.

Z or Third Variable

The importance of poka-yoke is to minimise errors by identifying a mistake. Ellsberg (1961) has shown that individuals express preferences for bets with known probabilities over bets with unknown probabilities. In order to minimise opportunity cost in any trade-off between variables X and Y, management have a third variable, Z, so that they are prepared to trade different pairs of X and Y provided Z remains at least constant in time period t and increases in time period t+1. Pairs of X and Y, for all n variables, $(X1,Y1) \ldots (Xn,Yn)$, translate into a business strategy: **more** profits and **less** revenues, or **less** costs and **more** profits. A business strategy requires action. Rational management prefer strategies yielding higher values for Z, and are indifferent between strategies yielding equal values. If by lowering costs in time period t management can realise a higher value of Z, then the observed strategy will be a lowering of costs. Keeping to type affords management a degree of certainty, a probability that the trade-off between X and Y will deliver a Z-result.

The Z-result is like a default outcome, which allows management to overcome the Penrose effect. Consequently, the Z-result is intricately linked to management type. The CEO is management of type Z. If player A is observed to choose Z (maximise value) **more often**, that is, with a higher probability than Z (maximise revenues), then this will have to be interpreted as an indication of his attaching a **higher utility** to it (Harsanyi, 1966). Within Framework Tn=3, there are a range of financial variables as candidates for X, Y and Z. The list is not exhaustive but includes revenues, price, profits, costs, R&D expenditure, dividends, value and profitability. There is also management utility. Management utility, U, a measure of satisfaction, is a key driver of the managerial models, but it is not the true utility as described in the neoclassical paradigm. Management utility is a **choice utility** as defined by Gul and Pesendorfer (2007), the determinant of behaviour, the explanation for why management opt to maximise growth or value or total revenues.

In other words, there is a personal satisfaction obtained by management in the realisation of an objective. In Figure 7.1, the pay-off in strategy A (action A) would be greater than the pay-off in strategy B (action B) if the non-zero CV was correct. Management are not surprised by the reaction of a competitor; although it is critical to be in a position to identify competitors, the **nearest rival**, that competitor who has the greatest probability of reacting first to one's action, is the main competitor. In other words, in a business framework described by technology and time, the identity of the nearest rival becomes more

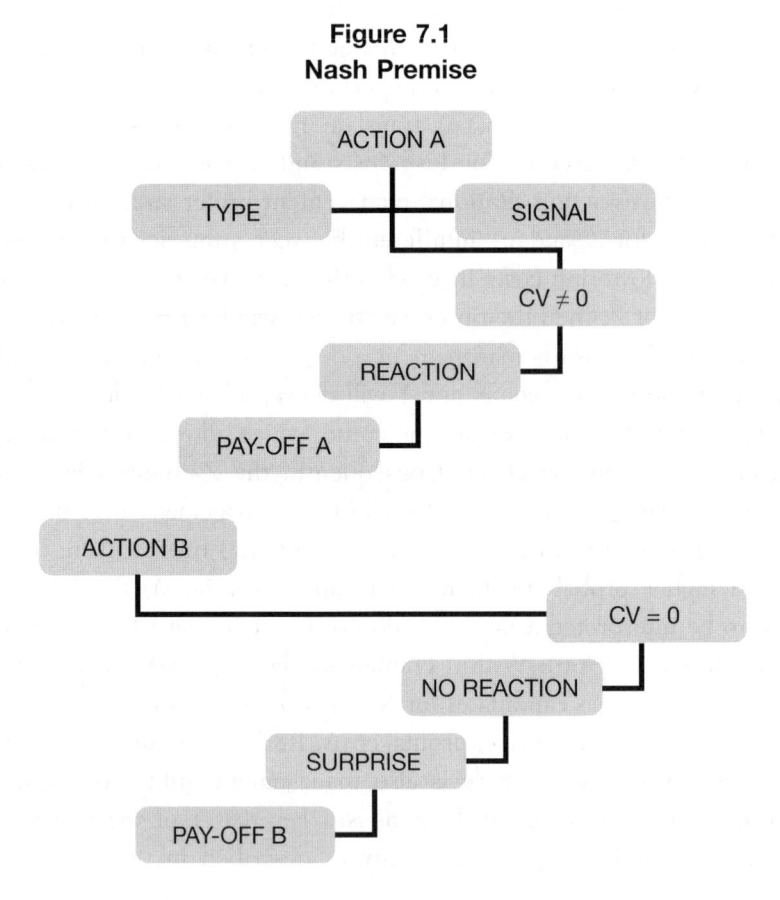

Figure 7.1
Nash Premise

```
                    ACTION A
        TYPE ───────────┬─────────── SIGNAL
                        │
                        CV ≠ 0
                        │
                    REACTION
                        │
              PAY-OFF A

ACTION B
    │
    └──────────────────────────── CV = 0
                                    │
                            NO REACTION
                                │
                        SURPRISE
                            │
                    PAY-OFF B
```

critical and more difficult in the absence of understanding signalling of player type. A first response would be to construct a critical timeline of competitor signals over a period of time.

Noise

Noise in a market is a distraction. McCullough describes noise in a game in terms of an error "when you might accidentally defect when you mean to cooperate or your partner will read your genuine cooperation as a defection" (McCullough, 2008). In Framework Tn=3 noise is a signal to get players to think x-way but to do y-way. When a player is in decline in time period t because of increased competition and shrinking demand, noise will exist in the market-as-a-game. In other words, one player may think x but do and signal y. When the rival reacts to y, believing that y is the opponent's true choice, the opponent plays x. Noise as a signal may manifest itself in a game where a player is playing not to lose rather than playing to win. In some respects this might explain Nokia's push into mobile services with maps and email, which was signalled in early 2007 with Ovi but officially launched in early 2009 as Ovi Maps and Ovi Mail. Ovi has been described in technology magazines as "a hub that integrates mobile services between handsets and PCs" (*The Economist*, 6 December 2008).

Nokia has a reputed worldwide market share of 40 per cent in handsets. In order to protect that market share – so that it does not fall, say, to 30 per cent – Nokia is creating noise by signalling a strategy that focuses not on growth of handsets per se but on the services it provides.

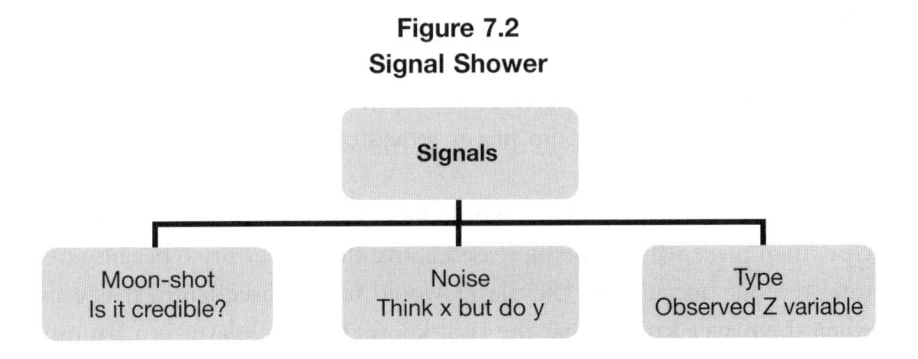

**Figure 7.2
Signal Shower**

```
                    Signals
                       |
      ┌────────────────┼────────────────┐
  Moon-shot          Noise             Type
Is it credible?  Think x but do y  Observed Z variable
```

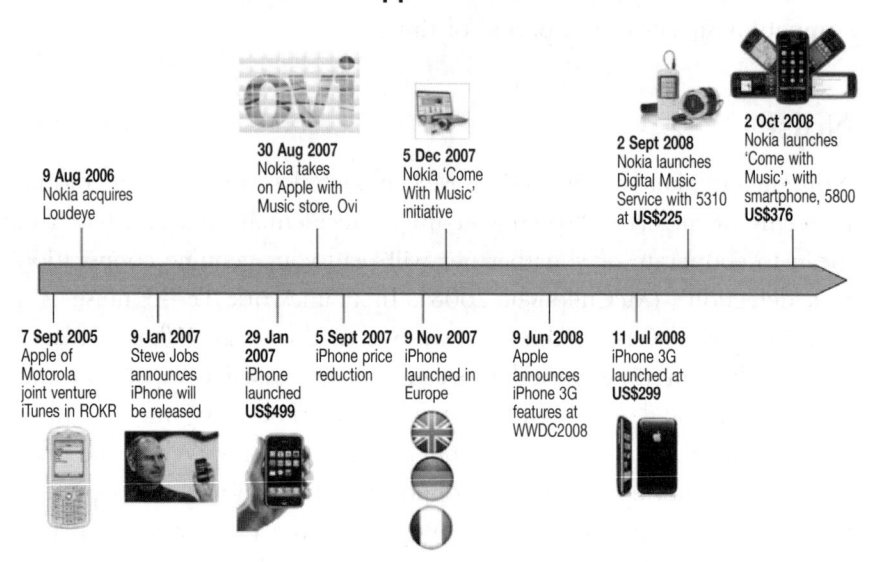

Figure 7.3
Critical Timeline: Apple with Nokia 2006 – 2008

- **9 Aug 2006** Nokia acquires Loudeye
- **30 Aug 2007** Nokia takes on Apple with Music store, Ovi
- **5 Dec 2007** Nokia 'Come With Music' initiative
- **2 Sept 2008** Nokia launches Digital Music Service with 5310 at US$225
- **2 Oct 2008** Nokia launches 'Come with Music', with smartphone, 5800 US$376

- **7 Sept 2005** Apple of Motorola joint venture iTunes in ROKR
- **9 Jan 2007** Steve Jobs announces iPhone will be released
- **29 Jan 2007** iPhone launched US$499
- **5 Sept 2007** iPhone price reduction
- **9 Nov 2007** iPhone launched in Europe
- **9 Jun 2008** Apple announces iPhone 3G features at WWDC2008
- **11 Jul 2008** iPhone 3G launched at US$299

Motorola's launch of the clamshell mobile phone design in the 1990s may well have been noise in the emerging game for dominance in handsets.

Noise in a Tumbling Price

In the market for mobile phones, both price and non-price characteristics are important in the game. Price falls can signal a Baumol type, and if players believe that there is a Baumol type in a game, price should not fall below the trigger price because net total revenue accruing to any player would fall. A rival, observing no price fall, believes that no player is a Baumol type. So no player reduces price and no player knows that there is a Baumol type, so no player moves on reducing price. This is a paradox.

If a player knows that the rival **believes** that the player is not a Baumol type, then price will not be increased above the trigger price because net total revenue accruing to the player would fall. Consequently, it is only when the player **knows** that the rival knows that the player is a Baumol type that the player will reduce price, but it is the action of reducing price (if present price is above the trigger price) that reveals the true identity of the player as a Baumol type.

Within the elastic range, a high prevailing price can be maintained to maximise profits in a concentrated market with fewer than five players. Any action by a player to reduce price (in order to recoup lost revenues) could be interpreted as a price signal from a Baumol type and is unlikely to precipitate a price reaction, if the rival knows that the player is a Baumol type, and price should only fall to the level of the Baumol type's trigger price floor.

Yet, if no player reduces price, prices will not tumble. For example, Nokia and Apple could succumb to this paradox of a tumbling price, in that as price falls in order to compete, the trigger price, activated by changing fickle consumer preferences for more functionalities, embeds a sequentially lower bound on the market price. As the game unfolds, the market price could fall to zero. The N97, for example, was launched in the UK in October 2008 at zero price. As that happens, a greater demand for functionalities is creating an inelastic demand that would warrant a price increase in time. Identifying patterns in observed signals is necessary in order for each player to isolate a rival's strategy as a string of price moves across the CTL. It is imperative that patterns are identified in the market-as-a-game, wherein innovation, rapid product development, technology and the demand for functionalities define the game dimension.

The significance of technology is reflected in the Apple versus RIM critical timeline in 2009. The competing products are differentiated by functionality (2G – 3G) but not by network. The market-as-a-game exhibits a range of observations, for example, Sony Ericsson smartphones target games fans, and in a bid to distinguish itself from rival mobile firms, Sony Ericsson is using PlayStation technology for its latest 2009 products. The HTC Touch is popular in Asia because it is cheaper than the iPhone and can be used on a variety of cellular networks.

94 Game Embedded Strategy

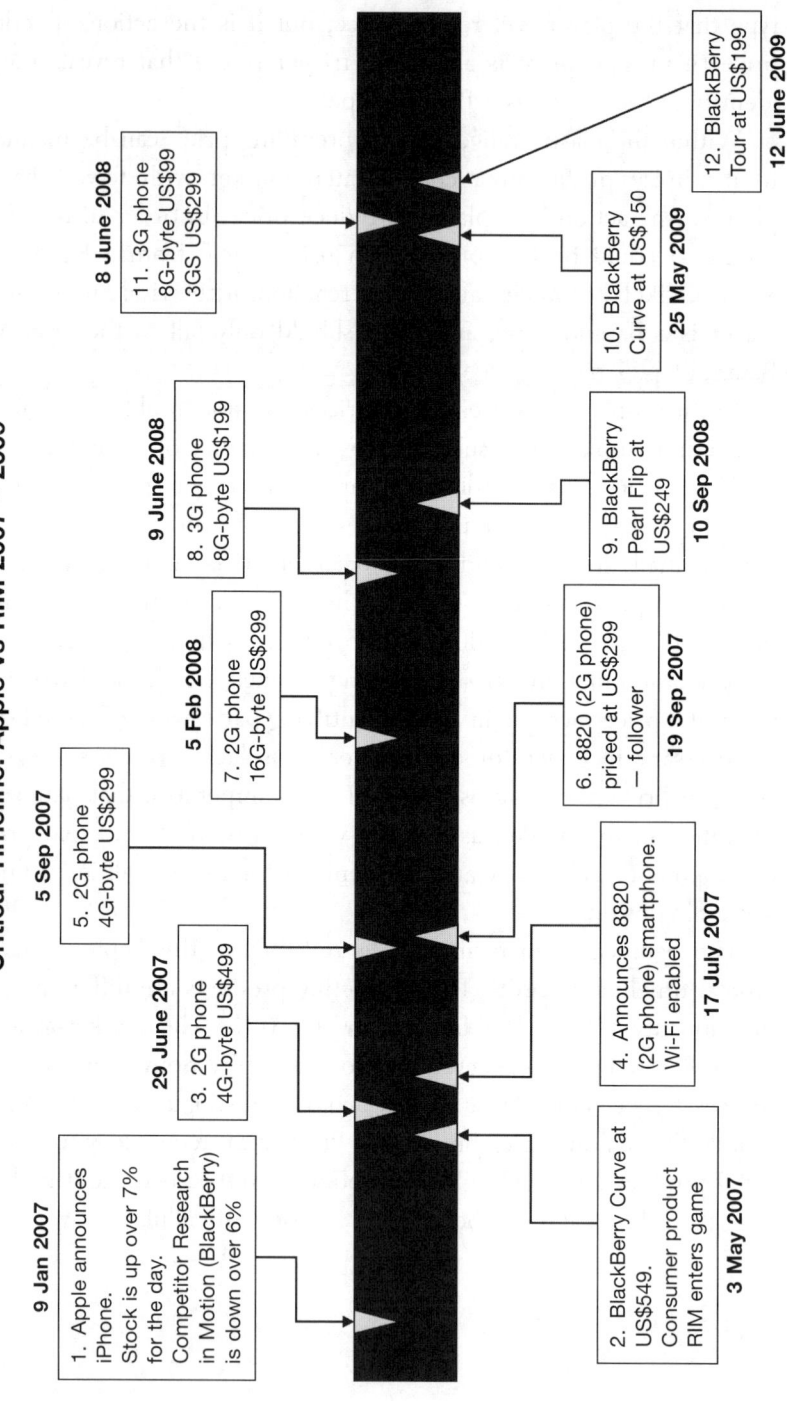

Figure 7.4
Critical Timeline: Apple vs RIM 2007 – 2009

9 Jan 2007
1. Apple announces iPhone. Stock is up over 7% for the day. Competitor Research in Motion (BlackBerry) is down over 6%

3 May 2007
2. BlackBerry Curve at US$549. Consumer product RIM enters game

29 June 2007
3. 2G phone 4G-byte US$499

17 July 2007
4. Announces 8820 (2G phone) smartphone. Wi-Fi enabled

5 Sep 2007
5. 2G phone 4G-byte US$299

19 Sep 2007
6. 8820 (2G phone) priced at US$299 – follower

5 Feb 2008
7. 2G phone 16G-byte US$299

9 June 2008
8. 3G phone 8G-byte US$199

8 June 2008
11. 3G phone 8G-byte US$99 3GS US$299

10 Sep 2008
9. BlackBerry Pearl Flip at US$249

25 May 2009
10. BlackBerry Curve at US$150

12 June 2009
12. BlackBerry Tour at US$199

The Mistakes of Dark Strategy

Management are used to dealing with incomplete information, and they make decisions daily out of uncertainty. Increasingly, new technology is presenting new challenges to management, and decision making is constrained by the kinetic equation $dT/dt = -1$. Across their suite of products and services there is at least one product or service market that is evolving into a market-as-a-game, and thus it behoves management to play the signalling game. Dark strategy facilitates mistake-proofing in the market-as-a-game that management already believe in, and the critical issue is the observed action of a competitor.

Strategy is a string of moves. Dark strategy refers to how management act, having observed the moves of a competitor while being aware that the competitor not only observes the action as a reaction but also knows that management are observing them. The sequence of observed moves can be plotted as a CTL as illustrated by Figures 7.3 and 7.4. The key to unlocking a sustainable competitive advantage is in determining a pattern in the observed moves, a pattern that management believe will be repeated if they act. By plotting a CTL as the game unfolds, management will see a pattern emerging, and they will see a string of moves that defines the strategy of a competitor. Management could also use the pattern to engage in a process called **backward induction**, whereby they plot, based on their belief system about competitors, the likely future outcome should they act now. It is as if Apple Inc in 2007 in Figure 7.4 could have predicted the likely reaction from Blackberry in 2008, and, with that knowledge in the market-as-a-game, play the game differently in 2007 to obtain a competitive advantage.

Near-rival Competitor

There are many competitors in the market but the one that is more likely to react first in the market-as-a-game is referred to as the near-rival competitor. Management who adopt dark strategy are **secure** in the market-as-a-game. Security in Framework $Tn = 3$ is ascribed to management who avoid the three mistakes of strategy. In a signalling game, secure management is convinced that they will persuade the competitor to choose the correct action and the competitor trusts the secure management sufficiently to act. The duration of the signalling cycle at $t = T$ will depend on whether Player B, the competitor, expects Player A to prefer Player B to act if signalled. A near-rival is that competitor who will not hesitate to act if its only alternative is to acquiesce with Player A. In other words, a near-rival is that competitor who, with positive probability, will react first at $t = K < T$ to the action from Player A at $t = K$. However, if at $t = K < T$, competitor C does not react and it is the case that Player A knows that the competitor C knows that reaction will **at least** lead to tumbling prices and a possible zero-price equilibrium at $t = T$, then Player A can assume that competitor C is not a near-rival at $t = K < T$.

First Mistake: Zero-Price Outcome

The type of a player that is signalled embodies some, but not all, of the decision-relevant private information. Player type is signalled by all players, allowing any one player to observe a common signal in the action of an individual player and to retain a private signal as noise or a moon-shot.

The private signal allows management the flexibility to react. Both technology and time are significant due to the curse of differentiation created by technology and the $dT/dt = -1$ kinetic equation respectively (see Chapters 1 and 2). A small but non-zero number of players of Bertrand type with $CV = 0$ proceed to reduce price in the belief that there will be no reaction from a near-rival – but there is a reaction. This is a mistake that reflects a lack of understanding of the game and could result in a zero-price equilibrium outcome. If a player incurs such a mistake, then the player could update their belief system on hindsight. To this mistake, dark strategy ascribes a solution in the origin of management beliefs.

Second Mistake: Failed Execution

A second mistake occurs with a Stackelberg type player with a non-zero CV but fails in the execution of the strategy. The executable strategy should weigh more in favour of the signals than any prior signal on observed action. Management are in a Bayesian game (Vives, 2005), when the weight attached by management to prior observed actions at t = T is greater than that attached to the signals at t =T. Bayesian type management see what they want to see and ignore the signals. To this mistake, dark strategy ascribes a solution in significance of signals.

The demise of Motorola's Razr is a good example of the second mistake, where Motorola management took the fashionable, highly inelastic US$400 Razr mobile phone in late 1990s early 2000 (t = K), mass produced it and flooded the market with it at a lower price. Sales fell sharply, although Motorola are in the ascendancy in 2009 with the recently launched Motorola Cliq.

Third Mistake: Lagged Differentiation

The third mistake of dark strategy occurs when management adopt new technology or product functionalities at time period t = K < T and they either rush to mass produce at t = T and the product fails or the firm experiences excess capacity at t = T when consumers baulk at the new product and sales fall below optimal production levels. Consumers have time-dependent preferences: they do not know what they want at t = T, but if it is available at time period t = K < T, then they will buy it but in insignificant numbers until the technology has gained an externality in use. To this mistake, dark strategy ascribes a solution in playing a game not to lose (second mover advantage) rather than in playing to win. With x per cent market share at t = K < T, a player plays not to lose in order to avoid (x − 1)% at t = T. Management, too, often play to win (x + 1)% at t = K < T, but end up with (x − 1)%.

CHAPTER 8

Homo Ludens

> "We can better satisfy our appetites
> in an oblique manner,
> than by their headlong and impetuous motion."
>
> **David Hume**

The central contribution of game theory to the economics of strategic management is a new language for the understanding of how to formulate and study strategic or inter-company optimisation involving two or more players. There is a wealth of applications in the literature, but we suggest that there are two fundamentally different classes of application of game theory to economic problems in business. The first is the application of two-person zero-sum games to primarily tactical business problems. The second is the application of n-person non-constant-sum-games to strategic issues involving threat analysis and price wars. It is this combined application of games that provides the genesis of the economics of strategy.

When our interests are confined to applications of the two-person zero-sum game, a reasonably strong case can be made for management as **Homo ludens** (game-playing man), as an intelligent, calculating entity with no personality or psychological foibles playing against an equally bloodless opponent. We can extend the concept of individual rational behaviour to the two-person zero-sum game. When our concerns are strategic and the game is naturally a non-zero mixed-motives optimisation, that is, where there is neither total coincidence nor total opposition of interests, the model of an individual actor may not suffice to capture the behaviour of the players. It is in this context that we have introduced the idea of a decision quantum in order to help differentiate between management as an individual and the management team working as a group and the different groups functioning as a product market. A host of assumptions concerning the players and their game environment may have to be introduced later in Chapter 9 in order to facilitate a model of some aspect of business reality for analysis.

Game-playing Man

It has been 50 years since the publication of the seminal work on the theory of games with the interesting essays and approach of both Schelling (1960) and Shubik (1960), who raised a series of questions concerning the application of an intermix of game theory and gamesmanship to strategic analysis. Further, the recognition of the need to study and formulate the principles of war dates back to the writings of Sun Tzu circa 500 BC. Although the seeds were sown many thousands of years ago, the specific development of a mathematical language for the study of conflict, cooperation and negotiation did not occur until the advent of the theory of games.

Notwithstanding the market structure, what is important for management is the degree of entry and their belief system on entrant types. Efficient entry is also best understood within the parameters of the type of competition that prevails in a market, including combat competition, scramble competition and contest competition (McNutt, 2005). It is best characterised by an efficient entry price. The efficient entry price is a long-run equilibrium price of entry.

Market Systems

Whether or not players in a market system cooperate and lock themselves into binding commitments, which may be caught by antitrust legislation, depends on the rules of conduct for player behaviour in a market system. McNutt argued that there is a Boolean network of player behaviour – at its simplest, it is a rule stipulating that each player acts on price if, and only if, two other players act. Player A makes a decision if two other players make a decision, but each player can decide to act or not at each decision point. In many respects it is about aggressive competition. Under scramble competition, for example, there is an exactly equal partitioning of the market and hence an equal division of the effects of competition between the competitors. Scramble may be manifested by changes in the size of players or in the number of players. Combat competition tends to be characteristic of more stable market systems where the acquisition of market share requires constant defence by the incumbent types.

If the market-as-a-game is played just once, allow for a unique pay-off of (2,2). It can be any number, but both players receive exactly the same amount. Each player knows exactly what they want to do (they have a dominant strategy), and each player has the easiest of decisions to face – keep prices high and receive 2. Both players would prefer to be in the top left cell of the matrix in Table 8.1, because in four cycles of this game a player could receive a pay-off of $8 = 2+2+2+2$. However, player A has a dominant strategy of competing to a low price, trying to do better by obtaining a pay-off of 3. But the 3 is obtainable only if player B continues to keep its prices high.

Table 8.1
Prisoners' Dilemma

		Player A	
		High p	Low p
Player B	High p	2,2	0,3
	Low p	3,0	1,1

In other words, if B keeps prices high, it is because he trusts A to do likewise and vice versa. So, B trusts A; but A, knowing that, betrays B. Once player B realises that player A has lowered its price, player B follows and they both find themselves in the lower right cell of the matrix with a pay-off of (1,1). A cartel between A and B might seem a solution, but with an inherent incentive to cheat or betray, enforcement of the cooperative solution might prove to be difficult, *vide* the arguments in McNutt, *Law, Economics and Antitrust*. Cartels may not last very long. If one player believes that the other player will always cooperate and keep prices high, then there is an incentive to betray or cheat. The issue is trust: If B keeps its prices high, can B really trust A to do the same? It is collectively that they both as players face a dilemma: How to obtain the cooperative outcome of 8 rather than the non-cooperative outcome of 6 or 4? Player A now ends up with $6 = 2+3+1+0$ or with $4 = 1+1+1+1$ if B punishes A for the betrayal by always keeping prices low. This is a recognised **punishment strategy**, signalling to A the pay-off 4 in time period $t+1$ instead of 8. In trying to do better, one can end up worse off! David Hume, an English philosopher writing in the 18th century, captured the idea: "We can better satisfy our appetites in an oblique manner, than by their headlong and impetuous motion." Remember that the future is not what it used to be!

Nash Equilibrium

In the exchange of prices, players interact with each other by using prices as signals. An incumbent and an entrant, or two incumbents, can face classic coordination problems. Conflicts can arise. In a two-person game, a pair of strategies will form a Nash equilibrium when each player cannot do better given the strategy the other player has adopted. A **Nash equilibrium** is a pair of strategies such that each is a best response to the other. The pay-off (1,1) in Table 8.1 is an example of a Nash equilibrium. To test whether a strategy combination forms a Nash equilibrium, just consider the following: let us call the strategy for the first player x* and the strategy for the second player y*. A pure strategy equilibrium is a Nash equilibrium in which the equilibrium strategies are played with certainty or with probability equal to 1. When the Nash equilibrium involves only strategies that are played with certainty, we have a pure strategy equilibrium. The alternative to a pure strategy equilibrium is a mixed strategy equilibrium in which, in equilibrium, each player adopts a strategy that selects at random from a number of pure strategies. For additional reading, refer to Dixit and Nalebuff, 2008: *The Art of Strategy*.

We need to ask whether, given that the second player will play y*, the first player can do better by switching to some strategy other than x*. Similarly, we need to ask whether, given that the first player will play x*, the second player can do better by switching to some strategy other than y*. If there is no better strategy for the first player than x* in response to the second player's y*, and if there is no better strategy for the second player than y* in response to x*, then this pair (x*, y*) is a Nash equilibrium for the game. McNutt, in *Law, Economics and Antitrust* looks at this scenario in terms of a semi-ordering of prices, where x* corresponds to a 'reduced' price by a defendant-firm and y* corresponds to a 'lower' price for an entrant-plaintiff. The pair (x*, y*) is aggressive pricing.

First Hurdle Initiative

When we raise the question of solution to a game, interesting issues arise between two-player games and n-person games. Dynamic games with few players, for example, have a leading contender in the perfect equilibrium, but it is not unique. For tactical problems involving two players, the saddle point or maximin-minimax solution provides a reasonable solution to a two-person game of opposition. Strategic problems have been considered primarily as games in extensive, strategic or coalitional form. Taking the first step in a game is crucial for management: if they take a first step and rivals follow, then management assume the mantle of leader. A volunteer is needed, but both players realise that if both of them volunteer, the worst possible outcome will obtain.

Both players have an incentive to volunteer given that the other player does not, and it is because of this incentive it can be argued that the precondition that the other player does not volunteer may not hold and hence to volunteer becomes the optimal strategy. The dilemma here is that it cannot be optimal for both players simultaneously, that is, the players do not have dominant strategies.

Unlike in the PD game, where there is a unique Nash equilibrium, in the Volunteer's Dilemma the solution can be characterised by either

Table 8.2
Volunteer's Dilemma

	S3	S4
S1	(2,2)	(2,3)
S2	(3,2)	(1,1)

one of the Nash equilibria (2,3) or (3,2). In the Volunteer's Dilemma, there is no strategy available by which one player can punish the other player for its deviation from a quasi-cooperative path.

Classic Prisoners' Dilemma

Earlier in this chapter we represented the possible outcomes to demonstrate the maxim of one player seeking to do better than (2,2) by obtaining a 3 but ending up at (1,1). The player can obtain 3 only if the other player receives 0. In other words, one player opts for a low price but only if a second player keeps its price high – that is the only way to secure a 3. But the second player soon realises that 0 is an outcome, so that player also reduces its price to low and both players end up at (1,1).

Table 8.3
Classic Prisoners' Dilemma

	High p	Low p
High p	[2,2] We can both have a 2 pay-off	[0,3] You want this 3 pay-off instead
Low p	[3,0]	[1,1] We both end up with a 1 pay-off

The only solution is communication, and this is illegal in the real world due to the antitrust legislation on cartels and price fixing. In other words, one player, a price leader, initiates an agreement to remain at the (2,2) outcome. In many markets, a fact finder would observe constant or fixed prices. However, the mere adherence to a fixed price is not sufficient evidence of belonging to a cartel, as there must be some evidence of a rule or mechanism to ensure that the (2,2) outcome obtains across all periods and there is no incentive to cheat because of, say, a punishment strategy.

If both players communicate over a four-period game, then the total pay-offs amount to $2+2+2+2 = 8$. If one player deviates from the agreement and cheats by charging a low price in the second period, that player obtains $2+3 = 5$. However, the other player observes the cheating behaviour and reduces its price to low and does not move in order to punish the first player who now obtains $2+3+1+1 = 7$ with a realisation of $1+1+1+1 = 4$ for all periods unless there is an agreement not to cheat. But this is difficult to maintain in the real world unless a credible punishment mechanism can be put in place by one of the players. Competition enforcement agencies now rely on whistle-blower legislation to entice a cartel member to come forward and reveal the cartel mechanism. Alternatively, with an incentive for a player to do better, any cartel is inherently unstable.

The Folk Theorem in game theory spells out the means by which firms can attain outcomes that appear collusive without necessarily engaging in overt collusion – or, indeed, even discussing together what to do. It shows how collusive outcomes can be attained 'as (sub-game perfect) non-cooperative equilibria' (Friedman, 2000). However, in producing cooperative behaviour from a conventional non-cooperative equilibrium, the Folk Theorem, it has been argued, blurs the distinction between explicit collusion and tacit collusion. From the standpoint of intent, this makes antitrust investigation rather delicate. In addition, it opens up consideration of partial collusion, wherein players collude on certain choices (prices) and not on others (location or markets) as argued by Friedman, Jehiel and Thisse (1995). It also leads to unintentional cooperation or the asymmetric sameness in price standard discussed in McNutt (2005) and later in this book.

Mixed Strategy

An example of a mixed strategy would arise if one player in an exchange of prices randomly decided to change or not change price with equal probability. This particular mixed strategy in a predatory pricing game may not be part of a Nash equilibrium. A national competition agency or court, for example, would need to discover the other firm's response to this strategy. The other firm would compute the expected pay-offs from each of the pure strategies of changing and not changing price. A national competition agency or court must try to comprehend whether management are acting rationally if they choose a strategy that does not maximise the firms' pay-off. Alternatively, a national competition agency or court must balance this with whether or not the management of an incumbent firm are willing to predate in order to convince entrants that they are aggressive rather than rational.

In the application to strategic business decisions, what is equally important for management is to understand the game, and the strategy may well depend on management's interpretation of the context in which they obtained the move or took the action. This is a classic dilemma in cartel pricing: if player 1 keeps prices high, both players get (10, 10) and the game is over. But it is player 1's move to keep prices high or not. If player 2 ever gets the move, then player 1 is either irrational or has made a blunder of some sort. If player 2 gets the move, he can end the game at a new pay-off or give the move back to player 1. Player 2's strategy will depend on the context in which the move was obtained.

Making decisions and taking actions can be understood only with reference to the subjective behaviour of management, so we find it useful to interpret decision making by differentiating between knowing that (making a decision) and knowing how and when to act (taking an action). The iconic Prisoners' Dilemma in games arises precisely because one player takes an action to break away from the agreed decision on the presumption at this point in time that the other player will not react. Paradoxically, while management may prefer to avoid conflict, individually they may prefer an outcome that can be obtained only by conflict. This is the conundrum embedded in the PD expressed as follows: in trying to do better than the status quo by taking an action, the individual ends up worse off. But someone has to take the first step, otherwise there is no game; there will be no market interaction.

Morphing into a Decision Quantum

Understanding type allows management as a player in a game to minimise a trial-and-error learning process in which they gradually discover that only some strategies work. Management at time period t do not have complete knowledge of details of the game. The market in which they are competing evolves into either a combat system, a contest system or a scramble system (McNutt, 2005). Consequently, management as an individual evolves in the market-as-a-game.

As they recognise the degree of interdependence, management type morphs into a decision quantum (DQ), a player, and the rules of the game, the type of players and the pay-offs become common knowledge. Nokia's completion of the purchase of Symbian in 2008 is an interesting example of management type morphing into a DQ. A signal to Apple, Google and Microsoft was sent in the summer of 2008 when Nokia completed the deal to buy out Symbian, the leading maker of operating system software for advanced mobile phones. The software is used in at least 50 per cent of mobile phones and is an integral part of delivering the functionalities of mobile music and photo sharing. The mobile market is evolving into services, and players have to ask: Will one operating system dominate in the handset market much like Microsoft Windows in the PC market? Much will depend on the game dimension: on other rival players such as Google's Android, BlackBerry, iPhone and Linux but also on the need for handset manufacturers to sign up for one software.

SMIN©

An engineering solution would change the rules of the game. Let us coin a new word and call a new 'want-to-have' product the 'small and thin (SMIN)'. This can combine the functionalities of a smart-phone with the functionalities of a netbook and it could offer a first-mover advantage to any player who first launches it to the market. However, if the new product is more like a netbook, then it may not fit neatly into the jacket pocket or purse; if the new product is more like a smartphone, it may have limited processing power or the screen may be too small to facilitate word processing. Whatever the dislike, consumers will not buy the product if it does not match their specific set of functionalities, so many players are prepared to wait and secure a second-mover advantage. In the interim, there is a risk that an unknown or smaller player might just get it right and capture that elusive first-mover advantage. But that is a judgement call for management as DQ to make and Framework $Tn=3$ complements the existing strategic toolbox deployed by management in making that call.

In 2009, Dell launched the Adamo (initially in China); Celio's Redfly C8N received mixed reviews on the launch; Acer displayed the M900 smartphone; and Nokia signalled entry into the laptop market. For small and thin devices like SMIN, the market-as-a-game represents an interesting example of an evolving market system in mobile devices. PC players and mobile phone players do see an opportunity but are cautious. There is history in the market-as-a-game from the 1990s *viz* Apple's Newton PDA failed, Dell's MP3 player and HP's line of televisions failed as products. Consumers with time-dependent preferences and changing demand for mobile devices are creating a challenge for the players in this market-as-a-game. An engineering solution may exist and potentially offer a DQ player a first-mover advantage. Mistakes can be costly. However, with changing demand and ever-changing new technology, mistake proofing is mandatory in order to at least predict the reaction of competitors and to prepare to react to the uncertainty created by type, technology and time.

CHAPTER 9

Market-as-a-Game

> "They came to the fields of joy,
> The fresh turf of the Fortunate Woods …
> Here was the company of those who had suffered
> Wounds fighting for the Fatherland."
>
> Aeneid, vi., 638, 660

The misreading of signals is one of the reasons for uncertainty in the business world. The market is introduced in terms of the market-as-a-game, focusing on the interaction of competitors as players in a product market wherein there is a recognised interdependence amongst the players. We do make some assumptions: **Assumption I**, player assumption, is that the company or firm is referred to as a **player** and this carries with it an understanding that the company or firm is in a game with other players. We are starting from the premise that firms are aware of their interdependence and management as players are mistake-proofing. Move and countermove ensue until both firms arrive at an equilibrating solution.

Market-as-a-Game

Some firms do not necessarily carry this understanding of a player as provided in this book, but they do compete, and compete aggressively, with each other. As long as management never perceive their interdependence, the outcome achieved is the outcome expected and not the outcome attainable. However, in different geographic markets, whether local, national or global, where the number of players is less than five there is a greater probability that the firms are players and that the management team do realise that they are in a game. This is the market known as oligopoly. **Assumption II**, the definition of game assumption, is that a group of companies realise that they are in a game whenever the fate of one company depends not only on its own actions but also on the actions of the rest of the companies in the market (Binmore and Dasgupta, 1986).

From a third-party perspective, a fact finder may observe play in a market by observing management behaviour and player actions, say, from signals on price, quantity or dividends policy. It is quite a different thing to infer the player types in a market by observing the behaviour of the management alone. So, for example, by ascribing types to the management of company X, the fact finder becomes bounded rational about the player type. The fact finder, by employing the principle known as Occam's razor, ignores the features of the economic theory that cannot be observed. He has limited ability to distinguish one type from another. So, instead, the fact finder uses experience and easy-to-process signals to sort the problem into a small number of categories. Once management realise that they are in a game, camouflage may take place — deliberate attempts to confuse the opponent — and then the type of management is subsumed within the type of player. Consequently, player type is more difficult to predict and thus to observe ex-ante in the blending of types.

In the late 1920s, the French mathematician Emil Borel wrote a series of articles to show how games, war and economic behaviour were similar activities in that they all involved the necessity of making strategic decisions. Borel's work gained the attention of economists, and the most significant achievement was the publication by Von Neumann and Morgenstern (1944). There was now a belief amongst economists and mathematicians that a full-fledged theory of games could be developed, providing a much better understanding of oligopoly behaviour than that offered by traditional economic theory.

In their seminal work, Von Neumann and Morgenstern introduced the fundamental classification of games into those of complete information and those of incomplete information. Competition may manifest itself in different ways, for example, in terms of price competition or advertising expenditures, but in a game we are focusing on patterns of observed behaviour. In this enriched view of a market, management embedded in a firm as a player will continue to look at prices but will also look at patterns of prices over a period of time; they may need to also look at entropy in the market shares (and in Chapter 10, we will discuss scramble, combat and contest competition).

Unlike formal games such as chess, bridge or poker, which have a well-defined beginning and ending, most models of strategic business situations cannot be easily assigned a clear end-point or rest point. In essence it becomes the responsibility of the fact finder to establish the context in which the game is played. The behaviour of management as described must be assessed in the context of the situation at hand. **Assumption III**, an assumption of symmetry, is deployed to capture the point that any differences in abilities of individual management must be specified within the model, otherwise all non-specified attributes are regarded as the same. The value of this assumption is significant as a device for simplification. For example, if we wish to apply the two-person zero-sum game to a price-revenue evaluation problem involving a task on elasticity, the assumption that the opposing players are equal in all respects appears to be reasonable. For example, as management they each understand the economics of the total revenue test: price increases on an inelastic demand will tend to increase net total revenues.

Homo Ludens

However, individual management, **Homo sapiens**, is limited in both the ability and capability to see, comprehend, process and act upon all the information available. His strategic cousin, **Homo ludens**, is to be regarded as a simplification of management with bounded rationality. In the study of threats, bargaining and negotiating as applied to management and business it may be worth considering, therefore, a blending of type of management with type of player into a decision quantum (DQ), the game-playing type analogue of a management team. The behaviour of the DQ is said to be rational only insofar as it coincides with an equilibrating behaviour. It is reasonable so far as the player has sound judgement. Consider the pay-off matrix from the game theory literature in Table 9.1.

The row player can play a if she can reasonably believe that the column player could play A, since a is a best response to A. She can reasonably believe that the column player can play A if it is reasonable for the column player to believe that the row player could play a. He can believe that she will play a if it is reasonable for him to believe that she could play a, etc. This provides an infinite chain of consistent beliefs that result in the players playing to an outcome (a, A). In the business application, it is critical that each player has a belief system conjectural variation and each action should be defined in terms of a CV (see Chapter 7). In other words, a Baumol type with a CV = 0 could reduce price to increase total revenue. Unless management as a player signal this type to the market, other players might interpret this price reduction as a threat and react by reducing price, and this tit for tat as illustrated in Figure 9.4 could continue until the signals are matched. Alternatively, a signal to the market that player X is a Baumol type will allow other players to believe that player X is a Baumol type and the observed price reduction is a one-shot price move requiring no reaction.

In Heinrich (2004), for example, social preferences are admitted to the Prisoner's Dilemma game, allowing for the possibility that some players are averse to inequality. It is argued that some players in a PD game prefer the more equal but personally less profitable outcome of mutual cooperation to the more asymmetrical pay-off produced by defecting against a cooperator. Within the PD pricing game once one player deviates by lowering price, Dp, there is a temptation for another player to follow. In other words, there is a kind of reciprocity in pricing as follows: My rival has introduced Dp; would it pay for me to do the

Table 9.1
Homo Ludens

	A	B
a	1,1	0,0
b	0,0	1,1

same? The reciprocal price may not be so easily forthcoming in business, as management are either increasingly subject to shareholder constraints or do not have the production capacity at a point in time to proceed with a matching price reduction.

Price Tumbles

Therefore, DQ1's perception of DQ2 will influence its decision to commit resources to either avoiding or precipitating a price tumble. Consequently, the reaction system has to be interpreted in such a way that the roll-out of DQ1's price – in retrospect, the history of DQ1's prices – is relevant for DQ2's action. The price reaction functions are linear and have a positive slope to indicate that a given price reduction from DQ1 (fixed amount of resources) is triggered by a given price reaction from DQ2. But this action-reaction is only possible over a limited amount of time before each DQ begins to read the signals from the game. The essence of the competitive process is trying to understand the complex web of competitors' behaviour. Reaction function allows management to track the price reactions of competitors. Management in a game under the zero-sum constraint will soon learn to weigh competitors' price reaction more than the limitations imposed on price by the own demand elasticity. This is the essence of strategic pricing.

'Price war' is a term used in business to indicate a state of intense competitive rivalry accompanied by a multilateral series of price reductions. One competitor will lower its price, and (in sequence) others will lower their prices to match. If one of the reactors reduces their price below the original cut price, then a new round of reduction is initiated. Price war is usually costly in terms of the opportunity cost of real resources used to defend market shares. Management should avoid price wars that are costly and erode into profits.

Bertrand Model

The focus here is on strategic complements in a highly differentiated oligopoly market. It is on likely price reactions in such a market. This model examines the pricing behaviour of interdependent companies in a product market with few competitors. This is more applicable to the oligopoly markets. Figure 9.1 shows non-intersection of the reaction functions of companies A and B. The price equilibrium is 0, at the origin. There is every likelihood that both players could drive the price to the (0,0) price equilibrium as the game will continue until the equilibrium price is reached.

Figure 9.1
Bertrand Zero-price Solution

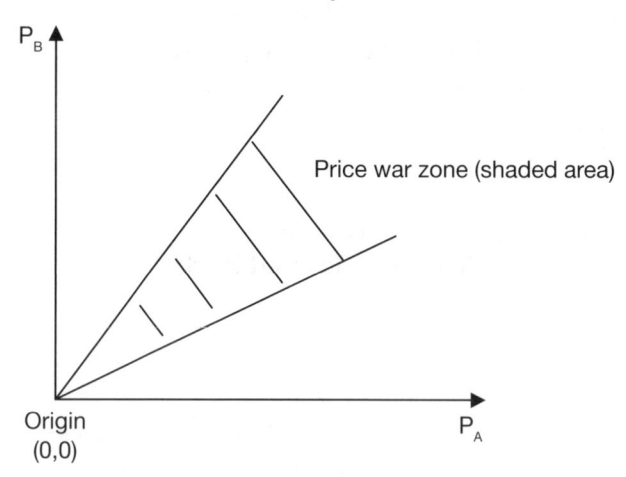

[Graph: P_B on vertical axis, P_A on horizontal axis, with a shaded wedge-shaped "Price war zone (shaded area)" emanating from the Origin (0,0).]

The challenge for the Bertrand model is to explain why (1) in some markets, in the absence of overt collusion, competing players are able to maintain high prices: e.g., the US cigarette industry in the 1990s; (2) in some markets where interdependence is acute, there is significant price competition: e.g., regional cement suppliers and the global video games market post-1998 and 2001–2005. The Sony-Microsoft game 2000–2004 is discussed in the following pages of this chapter.

Bertrand Challenge Explained By:

1. **Realisation of the Nash Equilibrium**
2. **Folk Theorem Benefit-Cost Condition**
3. **Asymmetric Sameness in Price Condition**
4. **Error in the Game**

Realisation of the Nash Equilibrium

We explore the first challenge in Figure 9.2 with intersecting reaction functions where the point of intersection is a Nash equilibrium price for both players. It is neither an equal price nor a profit maximising price, nor does it represent equilibrium where both players have equal market shares. It is the best outcome for each player given the reaction of the other player.

Figure 9.2 shows the intersection of the reaction functions of the companies. Price war occurs until the intersection point of the two reaction functions. That is the Nash equilibrium price. To see this applied to the Sony-Microsoft game dimension 2000–2004, refer to McNutt (2008).

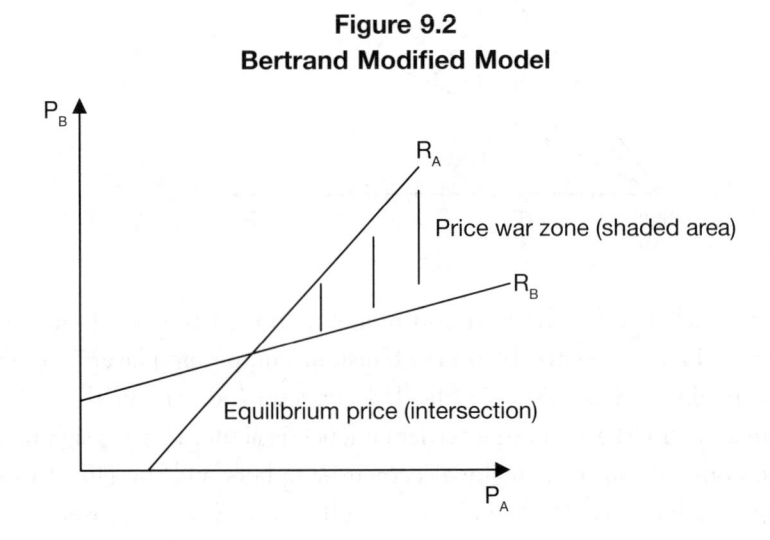

**Figure 9.2
Bertrand Modified Model**

P_B axis, P_A axis; reaction functions R_A and R_B; Price war zone (shaded area); Equilibrium price (intersection).

The process here is to observe the Nash equilibrium from the observed signals. It is at price point 149 and 149.99. This is the best price that both players could have achieved given the reaction of the other player. Management observe the signals ex-post and begin to reason strategically in a process called **backward induction** (see Chapter 7) by plotting the CTL and the reaction functions as illustrated in Figures 9.3 and 9.4 respectively.

Figure 9.3
Critical Timeline: Sony vs Microsoft

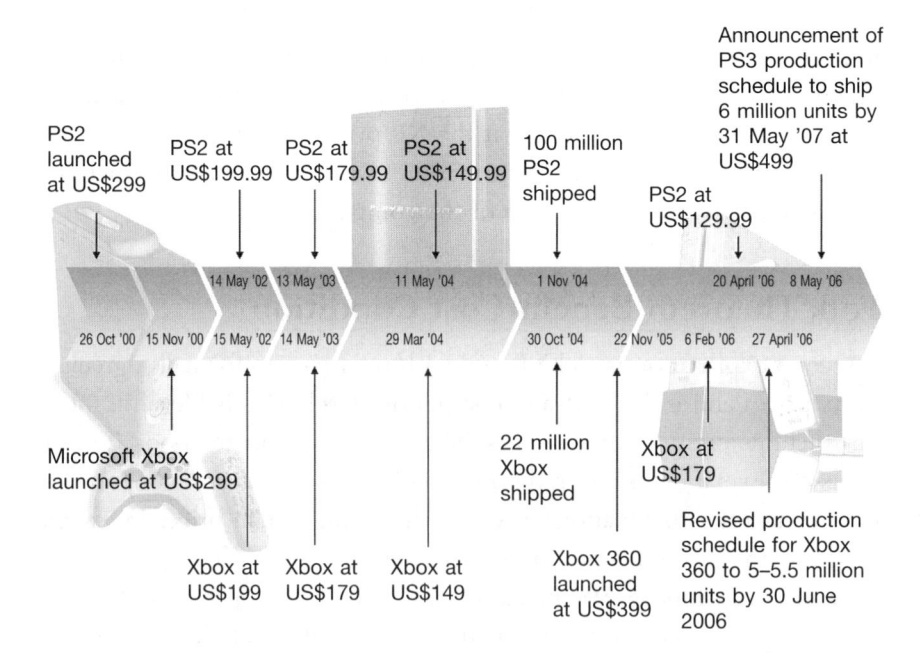

- PS2 launched at US$299 — 26 Oct '00
- Microsoft Xbox launched at US$299 — 15 Nov '00
- PS2 at US$199.99 — 14 May '02
- Xbox at US$199 — 15 May '02
- PS2 at US$179.99 — 13 May '03
- Xbox at US$179 — 14 May '03
- PS2 at US$149.99 — 11 May '04
- Xbox at US$149 — 29 Mar '04
- 100 million PS2 shipped — 1 Nov '04
- 22 million Xbox shipped — 30 Oct '04
- Xbox 360 launched at US$399 — 22 Nov '05
- PS2 at US$129.99 — 20 April '06
- Xbox at US$179 — 6 Feb '06
- Revised production schedule for Xbox 360 to 5–5.5 million units by 30 June 2006 — 27 April '06
- Announcement of PS3 production schedule to ship 6 million units by 31 May '07 at US$499 — 8 May '06

Figure 9.4
Nash Equilibrium: Sony vs Microsoft

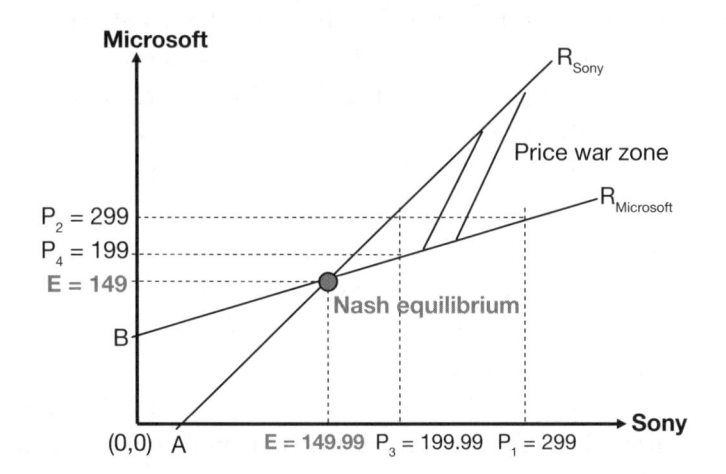

- $P_2 = 299$
- $P_4 = 199$
- $E = 149$
- $E = 149.99$
- $P_3 = 199.99$
- $P_1 = 299$
- R_{Sony}
- $R_{Microsoft}$
- Price war zone
- Nash equilibrium

If the fact finder were to inform both players at the price point 299, the history point, that (1) they were about to enter a price war and (2) the best price for each would be in the price range 149–149.99 after four years of price competition, neither player would believe the fact finder. This is the classic PD, as both players believe that they can do better. It is important to note that the NE price is not the best in terms of maximum profit or maximum market share; it is simply the best in the game play given the reaction of the competitor.

Folk Theorem Benefit-Cost Condition

A second explanation is to be found with reference to formally agreeing to fix prices above the Bertrand competitive level. This is illegal in most jurisdictions due to antitrust laws. The authors of this textbook do not focus on formal collusion; rather, the authors use the term 'cooperative pricing' to refer to situations in which firms can sustain prices in excess of those that would arise in non-cooperative single-shot games. Put another way, suppose two firms are unilaterally setting prices that are near the prices they would set if they successfully colluded. Are there conditions to do with costs and profits under which neither firm would wish to undercut its rival? Under these conditions cooperative pricing is feasible.

However, much remains unclear in the substitution of accounting profit for economic profit, particularly if, as noted by Demsetz, monopoly profits of the incumbent are capitalised in the accounting value of the firm's assets, notably, patents and trademarks. In most cases the only hard number is the market share, and the concepts of dominance and significant market power are defined with respect to a market share threshold. Landes and Posner argued for not defining market power in terms of specific market shares at all, but instead 'to interpret the market share statistics in each case by reference to qualitative indicia of the market elasticity of demand and the supply elasticity of the fringe firms'. They continued to argue that if either the market elasticity of demand or the elasticity of supply were high, different inferences would be drawn from the defendant's market share than if either or both of the elasticity values were low.

Asymmetric Sameness in Price Condition

An asymmetric sameness in price standard is asymptotically close to a bargained competitive price, and therefore it follows that not all instances of parallel behaviour can give rise to the same strength of inference that the parallelism results from anything other than the independent commercial judgement of the firms. Parties that engage in tacit collusion are behaving quite differently from firms that enter into explicit cartels. Management of firms that engage in tacit collusion may not even know what they are doing; they may not recognise that the pricing practice helps to support an anti-competitive equilibrium. In many markets, price can take on its own momentum: for example, demand for a limited supply will increase price under the basic law of supply and demand. Conversely, in a competitive price environment, price will fall to a low price on its own momentum.

Consider two outcomes: incumbents having excess capacity that signals a threat to new entrants; and a market with excess capacity that is not attractive to enter. A combination of the two outcomes could mean that we are dealing with a mixed duopoly where both firms simultaneously decide whether to enter the market or not and to communicate this, and eventually they play a Cournot-Nash duopoly game choosing the output. Barros (1984) has shown that a mixed duopoly may indeed lead to an improvement in allocative efficiency. For a fact finder trying to understand the proper context of type of competition in a market, the actions and reactions of the firms should be regarded as an evolving process in which each participant carries out its duty in the market, the job in which each is more efficient. The basis of any 'understanding' is an increase in market power with a concomitant increase in allocative efficiency.

Competition or antitrust law and policy is about maximising consumer welfare, and that can be achieved only by lower competitive prices at the retail level. The perfectly competitive price that competition promises continues to elude the consumer across many product and service markets. If we begin with the premise that a market is a classic case of signalling wherein the ability to 'do a deal' and negotiate or conduct transactions at prices through signalling mechanisms may be the modus operandi, then the fact that a bargaining mechanism – cartel arrangements or signals – exists at all reflects the nature of the business, and the fact that a bargaining mechanism cannot easily be monitored by others would make it difficult to detect instances of alleged price fixing.

Error in the Game

A price signal, Δp, from one player may not always lead to a matching price reduction. Furthermore, it does not require an immediate Δp if the player has a commitment to altruistic behaviour. Once the first player observes that the second player is not following with a Δp, the first player may stop and reconsider the Δp. If so, the second player has influenced the first player not to initiate Δp, in effect changing the behaviour of the first player. In these circumstances, fact finder would observe cooperation and proceed to dismiss the possibility that it could have emerged from nothing more than the cold calculation of self-interest. It need not necessarily rely on a credible mechanism.

One important signal for DQ2 is the intention of DQ1 in initially reducing the price: Was the intention to make a price war unavoidable, using it as a catalyst for greater competition? DQ1 with a CV = 0, for example, could be interpreted as a naïve strategy, especially once DQ2 reacts with a price reduction. Both DQs find themselves in a price war, but DQ2 would have to ask: Did DQ1 intend to initiate a price war? This is the error in the game – the incomplete information that can trigger a price war. And it also raises the time constraint – whether any DQ has a binding time constraint within which to complete the action.

With error, DQ1 may have a lower bound on price – thus facilitating intersecting reaction functions – otherwise DQ2 might believe that DQ1 is moving to the zero-price equilibrium. If DQ2 is going to follow with a price reduction (as perceived by DQ1, that is, CV $\neq$ 0), there is no reason why DQ1 should initiate a price war; and conversely if DQ2 has CV $\neq$ 0 then DQ2 will not initiate a price war. The price tumble that triggers a price war scenario is more likely to manifest itself with asymmetric information, where one DQ is informed of all the parameters but a second DQ is not informed as to a competitor DQ's aversion to a price war or willingness to engage.

It depends on how the DQ views the pay-offs in the game. There is an element of regret in not taking an action. The costs of regret would have to factor in the costs of playing the game. This is discussed in McNutt (2008). In Table 9.2, assume you are player A with two strategies, S1 and S2. Player B has two strategies, S3 and S4. You play S1 only if the pay-off of 3 is the maximin. If you are player B, and if player A has played S1, you play S3 only if the pay-off of 4 is your minimax.

Table 9.2
Regret Matrix

	S1	S2
S3	3	4
S4	5	1

The Regret Matrix

Within Framework $Tn = 3$, we are advocating that it is more rational for business management as players to think in terms of the opportunity costs rather than the gains in a pay-off matrix. Consider a player faced with three options, S1, S2 and S3. The player has a conjectural variation. For illustration purposes, the pay-offs are defined in Table 9.3.

Table 9.3
Maximin

Action	CV = 0	CV ≠ 0	Minimum	Maximin	Maximum	Maximax
S1	10	1	1		10	10
S2	9	3	3	3	9	
S3	5	3	3	3	5	

Faced with a decision, management assuming the minimum pay-off may take a pessimistic view of the market-as-a-game. Therefore, they should act to ensure that they get as large a pay-off as possible in the market-as-a-game. This is called the maximin, because it maximises the minimum pay-off. So management are faced with two choices, S2 and S3, and they are indifferent between them. This is sometimes called the criterion of pessimism, in that the worst is always assumed. Alternatively, management may be an optimist and thus choose the maximax strategy, which maximises the maximum pay-off, leading to the selection of S1. Note that different criteria lead to different choices. If this were not true, then, as argued by Moore and Thomas (1976), "all criteria would lead to the same action suggesting that we might as well use a pin to pick out criterion" (p. 44).

But there is a third criterion that looks at the opportunity cost of choosing a strategy. It is referred to as the regret criterion, illustrated by pay-offs in a regret matrix. To understand this better, we convert the original pay-off from Table 9.3 into Table 9.4.

Table 9.4
Regret Criterion

Action	CV = 0	CV ≠ 0	Maximum Regret	Minimum of Max. Regrets
S1	0	2	2	
S2	1	0	1	1
S3	5	0	5	

If CV = 0 is correct in retrospect, then choosing S1 would have been the correct choice and management would incur no opportunity loss or regret as measured by the difference between the pay-off for the chosen strategy and the pay-off for the optimal strategy S1 with CV = 0. If the game is unprofitable to player A, player A should always use a maximin strategy. In other words, if player A cannot hope to obtain **more** than his maximin pay-off anyhow, then player A should adopt a strategy that will absolutely assure the player at least that much (Harsanyi, 1966).

In the mid-1990s Motorola was emerging as a significant player in the mobile phone market, a nascent market that has grown exponentially over the past ten years. In many countries there are more mobile subscriptions than people. But in retrospect, Motorola had CV = 0 with respect to a small obscure Canadian start-up called Research in Motion (RIM), who were targeting a new mobile email market. Had RIM, *aka* BlackBerry, not succeeded, then Motorola would have had no regret in their choice of strategy that underestimated the mobile email market potential.

Saddle Point Market Shares

If the game considered is a zero-sum game, strictly adversarial between the players, then maximin-minimax provides a unique stable equilibrium solution to the game. In many markets, the market shares are consolidated in the sense that should one firm gain 2 per cent it translates into a 2 per cent loss for one or more competitors in the market. The game is about market shares, and this is not an unreasonable assumption to make across many product markets for two-player games.

Consider two players, A and B, in Table 9.5. Assuming that player A has the strategy set (S1, S2, S3) represented across the rows and that player B can react with strategies (S4, S5, S6, S7) represented in the columns, then what should player A do if faced with the market share pay-offs? If player A could be sure that player B would respond with S4, S1 would be an optimal strategy for player 1 since it would get 95 per cent of the market. Strategy S1, given player B's response of S4, yields the largest pay-off for player A but the worst pay-off for player B, so player A can be certain that player B will not respond with S4.

Player A must assume that player B will respond with S5, which will give player B 95 per cent leaving player A with only 5 per cent. By assuming the worst possible response, player A predicts the outcome for his use of strategy S1 will be the minimum pay-off, that is, 5 per cent of the market. We illustrate this in **bold** print in Table 9.5. It would

Table 9.5
Saddle Point Matrix

	S4	S5	S6	S7	Row Minimum
S1	95	**5**	50	40	5
S2	60	70	**55**	90	55
S3	30	35	30	**10**	10
Column Maximum	95	70	55	90	

appear reasonable for player A to reject S1 as too risky. As viewed by player A, the strategy offers an almost all-or-nothing gamble. It depends on how player B responds. So player A chooses another strategy. S2 offers the possibility of 90 per cent if player B can be counted on to respond with S7. However, there is also the possibility that player B will respond with S6, allowing player A 55 per cent market share. This is the least market share for player A if he uses S2, so again we print it in **bold**.

If player A considers S3, the least market share is 10 per cent, obtained if player B responds with S7. Player A notes the least attractive outcome for each strategy. Player A in a zero-sum games assumes that the rival player B will deploy a strategy that reduces player A's market share to a minimum. So player A uses a **maximim** strategy, that is, the maximum of all the minima, and that is S2. Conversely, player B will select the highest possible outcomes in terms of player A's pay-offs providing column maxima of 95, 70, 55 and 90, as illustrated in *italics*. So in order to obtain the highest market share, player B will choose a strategy that will hold player A to the lowest of the greatest possible outcomes.

Accordingly, player B will choose S6, which allows player A 55 per cent market share. Confining player A to the least of the greatest shares, player B is said to be employing a **minimax** strategy, that is, choosing the minima of the column maxima. We conclude that the game does have a unique equilibrium. The market share **55** per cent is both the maximum of the row minima and the minimum of the column maxima. If player A chooses S3, player B will respond with S6; and if player B decides on S6, player A will reply with S2. The market share **55** per cent is referred to as the saddle point of the game.

Games in strategic or extensive form are obvious candidates for management games where player 2 is committed to not exciting a price war and player 1 either considers exciting a price war or not. Player 2 then faces the option of a counter-strike if a price war ensues. In this case, the non-cooperative solution is the dominant solution used to analyse games in strategic or extensive form. The main property of the non-cooperative equilibrium is optimal response. If A knows B's action, then at the non-cooperative equilibrium, A will have no desire to change his strategy as he cannot improve. The same holds for B. This gives rise to the Nash equilibrium, the best outcome a player can obtain given the moves or actions of other players.

The Core of the Bertrand Dilemma: Trust

Do you trust your partner? Should you trust your competitor? Trust ultimately depends on one's belief structure about other people, whether they be competitors or not, in the business world. If Mr A trusts Mr B to do x, then Mr B, knowing that Mr A trusts him to do x, has a choice to make: Does he do x, or not? The consequences of x are of interest in the business world. One scenario, referred to as the moon-shot, is the belief without providence that x will be done. Neither Mr A nor Mr B issued the moon-shot, neither knows that about the other, and so they behave as if the moon-shot has happened. Another scenario is the extent to which trust is credible in terms of doing x, where x has significant negative consequences for both A and B. In this cartel scenario, both players must trust each other absolutely.

Combat competition is about entry at the margin and manifests itself when an increasing number of firms is not an advantage to the market system. Contest competition differs in that the market is unequally partitioned – some firms are content with their market shares, while other firms are targets of merger or takeover. Contest would occur, for example, where individual firms compete either for a given market share or for market position. Contest competition can be seen as a mechanism that will tend to maintain the market level of concentration as long as the number of firms does not change. One essential characteristic of contest and scramble is that in both cases there is no exit of firms below a threshold level of concentration when there is ample market share for all competing firms.

Above a critical threshold level of concentration, exit increases abruptly in the case of perfect scramble but gradually in the case of perfect contest. This follows necessarily from the requirement that contest leaves a constant number of firms in the market system. We contend that almost all competition under normal market conditions falls between these idealised extremes of contest and scramble. This may be a key contributor to undermining an understanding in antitrust analysis that competition and concentration are antithetical. Within antitrust folklore, concentration leads to collusion; if we accept that competition and concentration are not antithetical, the debate in antitrust circles on concentration and collective dominance would become uncomfortable and possibly untenable, if it leads to the conclusion that competition contributes to collusion in a market system. However, it may be possible, theoretically at least, to enunciate the possibility of competition with monopoly outcomes. Pure contest is rare; as individual firms compete for market share, there will often be a compromise as combat competition becomes more intense and average market share may be reduced.

Stigler's Dilemma

Players avoid price wars. They are expensive. One option is to form a cartel. Stigler argued that firms seek cartelisation – the gains from cartelisation include a less elastic demand curve and a slower rate of entry. It is rational and may be commercially sound for modern firms to collude, and therefore no amount of legislation will stifle that desire. In US antitrust, parallel pricing arises under Section 1 of the Sherman Act, where the courts focus attention on the type of evidence 'from which a conspiracy can be inferred'. In this instance the type of behaviour referred to is conscious parallel behaviour. However, as we know, the difficulty in antitrust is in deciding whether or not parallel behaviour is sufficient to establish an agreement. A not dissimilar debate took place in EU competition circles arising from the court's interpretation of collective or joint collusion in the Gencor/Lonhro case (McNutt, 2005). The argument can be traced back to Sraffa (1926), who argued that firms would avoid competition if the expected rents from cartelisation exceeded the gains from long-run competition. This requires us to focus on the type of competition in a market and not on market structure per se, on scramble, combat and contest competition. Or alternatively, if management enter a signalling game, the risk of competition could be avoided.

Across the literature, it is clear there is a need to return to an understanding of the type of competition that prevails in a market under scrutiny with a focus on firms interacting in an evolving Boolean network of interrelated firm behaviour. As the atomistic behaviour of a perfectly competitive market structure leads to a long-run equilibrium, likewise the Boolean behaviour of the market systems evolves into an ordered arrangement that manifests itself as market-sharing strategies and inevitably implicit or parallel collusion on price. In types of market systems, the firm is an integrated network of market systems. As argued elsewhere, greater emphasis should be placed on the relevant firm than on the relevant market for antitrust analysis.

With different elasticities, for example, a two-firm and a ten-firm market structure challenge the traditional economic theory underpinning antitrust policy. A ten-firm structure with an industry elasticity of 0.5 could be more monopolistic as measured by the Lerner Index than a two-firm structure with an industry elasticity greater than 1.5. In the Chamberlin model, the degree of industry elasticity determines the level of profit. Could we imagine an industry structure that exhibits an oligopoly structure with zero long-run profit? The problem is that the industry structure is defined within the traditional structure-conduct-performance model with reference to H and η and deriving the equation

$$L = H/\eta$$

But this equation does not depend on any form of explicit collusive behaviour. Rather, the monopoly power arises from the exogenous assumption of Cournot-Nash play and the restriction on entry — these conditions assure an outcome, which, according to Cubbin (1988), could be interpreted as an 'apparently collusive arrangement'. Ironically, the monopoly equilibrium arises from the best-reply responses in what is essentially a non-cooperative Cournot-Nash competition.

Trigger Price

An equally important determinant is the DQ's knowledge about elasticity for its suite of products. At its simplest, elasticity measures the responsiveness of any quantity variable Δq to changes in price, Δp. The concept can be expanded to include supply-side responses and indeed to consider other quantity-type variables on the demand side. The most interesting is the advertising elasticity of demand, which would measure, for example, how a percentage change in advertising expenditure would contribute to changes in sales. This has been referred to earlier in the book as price elasticity (of demand). For a given linear demand, an elastic region lies above the mid-point and an inelastic region below the mid-point. The real market price will be in one or the other of the two regions. Therefore, strategically, DQ should now interpret a price fall as movement towards the mid-point and a price increase as a movement upwards towards the mid-point. How do we distinguish between the two? We can do so by computing that mid-point, the trigger price, and identifying the likely responsiveness in the direction of the price signal.

In the elastic region, as price falls sales increase, so revenue goes up; conversely, revenue falls if price rises. Therefore, in the elastic region, price and revenue are inversely related. By contrast, in the inelastic region, price and revenue are positively related. Now a management decision to change price must assume knowledge of such a price, the trigger price, because if price is to drop, it can do so only from the elastic range toward the mid-point, otherwise management fail the total revenue test. And such failure is a strategic mistake if the price change excites a price war by sending the wrong signal to rival players. If anything, the need to compute the trigger price is to act as a guide. It is not a real price that can be charged to consumers; rather, it is a measure of the amount by which a price **ought** to change in any price sequencing.

What Market to Enter?

Chandler's thesis is that structure follows strategy. In other words, it is the behaviour of management, observed as strategy by competitors, that determines the market structure. If a firm's strategy is to be carried out, or implemented, individuals working within the firm must know about the strategy and its operational requirement for tasks and actions, and their coordination. How the firm responds to problems of information, innovation, coordination and commitment in a game will determine its long-term position in an industry.

Within Framework $Tn = 3$, there is a game embedded strategy (GEMS) that has the following important characteristics. In particular, determining the preferred market will depend on a host of factors discussed throughout the book, from sustaining competitive advantage to strategic positioning in the market and playing the non-cooperative game of competition. Management's best response will ultimately depend on the unique set of circumstances they face, although management may differ by type and may differ on the threats facing the firm or how the firm should respond.

Dell Inc represents an interesting case. Competing on non-price attributes is a new approach for Dell and takes them into new strategic territories.

Figure 9.5
Dell's Movement in Strategic Focus

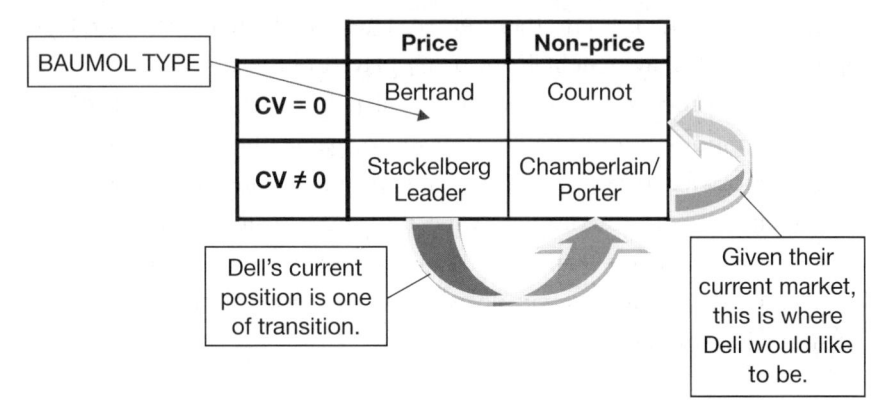

BAUMOL TYPE		Price	Non-price
	$CV = 0$	Bertrand	Cournot
	$CV \neq 0$	Stackelberg Leader	Chamberlain/ Porter

Dell's current position is one of transition.

Given their current market, this is where Dell would like to be.

All players would like to significantly differentiate themselves to remove their nearest rival from the horizon. In Dell's current strategic position, this could mean moving to the non-price competitive Cournot box with CV = 0. However, Dell Inc historically has a type – a Baumol type – of using price to drive earnings, revenues and value, and whether or not they keep to type can be gleaned from signals in CEO statements and through their fiscal year performance.

Drawing on Framework Tn=3, game theory can be used to directly play out scenarios to determine which strategic options are optimal. This is important for making the step from strategic option to strategic decision. The toolbox presented in this monograph can apply to business strategy at different levels – corporate, divisional or regional – all of which have one starting point: the goals of the organisation. Once the goals are known and understood, management seek to implement strategies that will achieve those goals. Tactics determine how each of the strategies is played out on a day-to-day basis. The toolbox incorporates game theory. There are many industry analysis tools and many models for deriving business strategies, including Porter's 5 Forces model and the Value Net. They can be deployed to support a view of the organisation with management as players in a dynamic non-cooperative evolutionary game.

The toolbox is a process that starts with requiring DQs to understand organisational goals. It then moves on to requiring an understanding of the industry in which the company operates and the factors affecting the industry and its future. Through this analysis, opportunities and challenges should present themselves. These in turn present strategic options, which may benefit from being played out as a game – the next stage in the process. Game scenarios will help determine which of the strategic options is optimal. Furthermore, game theory can help add insight into what factors are important in undertaking the chosen strategy, such as where to compete, what the price sensitivity of the market is, and how the firms structure themselves to compete effectively. The process ends with a strategic decision being made, given the outcome of strategic game playing.

A Game Embedded Strategy (GEMS)

Strategy Question: What Market Should We Be In?

A company should NOT be in a market where the identity of the nearest competitor is not known OR where the identity is known but not the likely reactions.

Dimensions of GEMS

Profits are captured by management as players. Porter's 5 Forces strategy focuses on the threat to industry profits, Framework $Tn=3$ identifies new opportunities for growth, and a game embedded strategy enables management to act to capture and retain profits in $t+1$.

A game embedded strategy is more likely to be ahead of the game in terms of the next strategy adopted in oligopoly markets. It facilitates a second mover advantage, and with no surprises a first mover advantage is obtained.

Participation in a game requires management to pay attention to signals, to camouflage their type and to be both consistent and coherent over the life cycle of the game.

Business strategy can be interpreted as games of complete information wherein management not only know their own type but also the type of the other competitors. Incomplete information is introduced by the concept of vertical blending, whereby the type of management blends with the type of player, and thus the preferences of management are clouded. In this context, by adapting the arguments of Harsanyi (1967, 1968), we are able to assume that each player has a particular characteristic, which determines its preferences over actions (social states) and its beliefs about the Z-preferences of the other players, the competitors.

In other words, with vertical blending the type of player is no longer common knowledge in the game. To have assumed that the beliefs of players are common knowledge in the real world of business strategy appears unreasonable. In reality, we have little idea how individual management actually acquires beliefs. However, vertical blending allows us to define the players in a game by their strategies. In other words, we do not ask: How does management behave? Rather, we ask: Given their strategy, how should they behave? The focus is on answering: What market should they be in? There is less focus on answering: How can they optimise in the present market? Management make a decision knowing that something has to be done in terms of improving financial performance, and then management take an action knowing how and when to improve that performance. The action depends on their understanding of type and their realisation that their company is a player in a market-as-a-game.

**Figure 9.6
Nomenclature on Type**

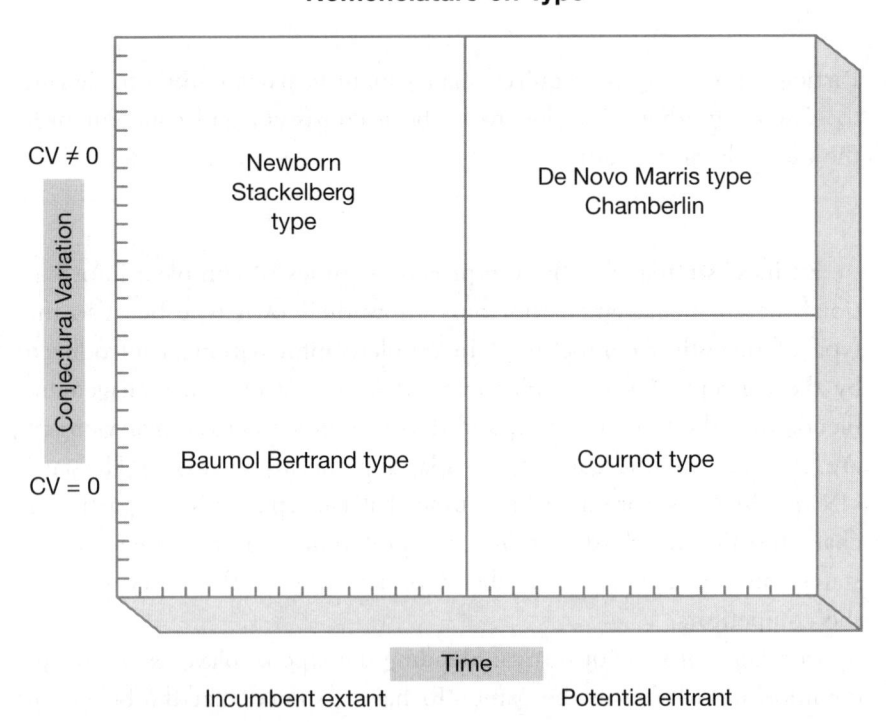

	Incumbent extant	Potential entrant
CV ≠ 0	Newborn Stackelberg type	De Novo Marris type Chamberlin
CV = 0	Baumol Bertrand type	Cournot type

Conjectural Variation (vertical axis); Time (horizontal axis)

GEMS Strategy Toolbox

In all the pay-off matrices, self-interest (maximising the size of the pay-off) governs the likely response of a player and the fact that the probability of the outcome is not relevant can be diluted through the introduction of behavioural characteristics of players. In assessing the game dimension, management should pay particular attention to understanding the behavioural characteristics of players in the game, as well as their type, and assessing the likely responses of players based on a set of assumptions, beliefs and prior knowledge. The key point to note is that game pay-offs can be adjusted to reflect the nature of the response by players, given assumptions made about their behaviour. Management should derive a set of behavioural aspects about the other players in a strategic game in order to factor in the likelihood that the behaviour will affect the game pay-offs.

The majority of pay-offs in the game analogies referred to in this book can apply and be extended to include conditional probability. Through the review of the concepts of game theory, it is clear that the discipline can add a different perspective and complementary approach to examining strategic business decisions. Many of the key elements of game theory provide insights into areas such as competitor reactions, pricing, cooperation and competition, the importance of scale, the value of information, signalling and the importance of communication. The concepts of adverse selection and signalling provide valuable direction and insight on how to compete. Game theory broadens the scope of economic analysis.

Easterbrook and McNutt have constructed a strategic toolbox to incorporate game theory (see Table 9.6). Game theory can be used to directly play out scenarios to determine which strategic options are optimal. This is important for making the step from strategic option to strategic decision.

It is critical to understand the future implications of one's action in time period t. One is reminded of Goethe, who tells us that Faust lost the liberty of his soul when he said to the passing moment, "Stay thou art so fair".

Table 9.6
Easterbrook–McNutt Strategic Toolbox GEMS

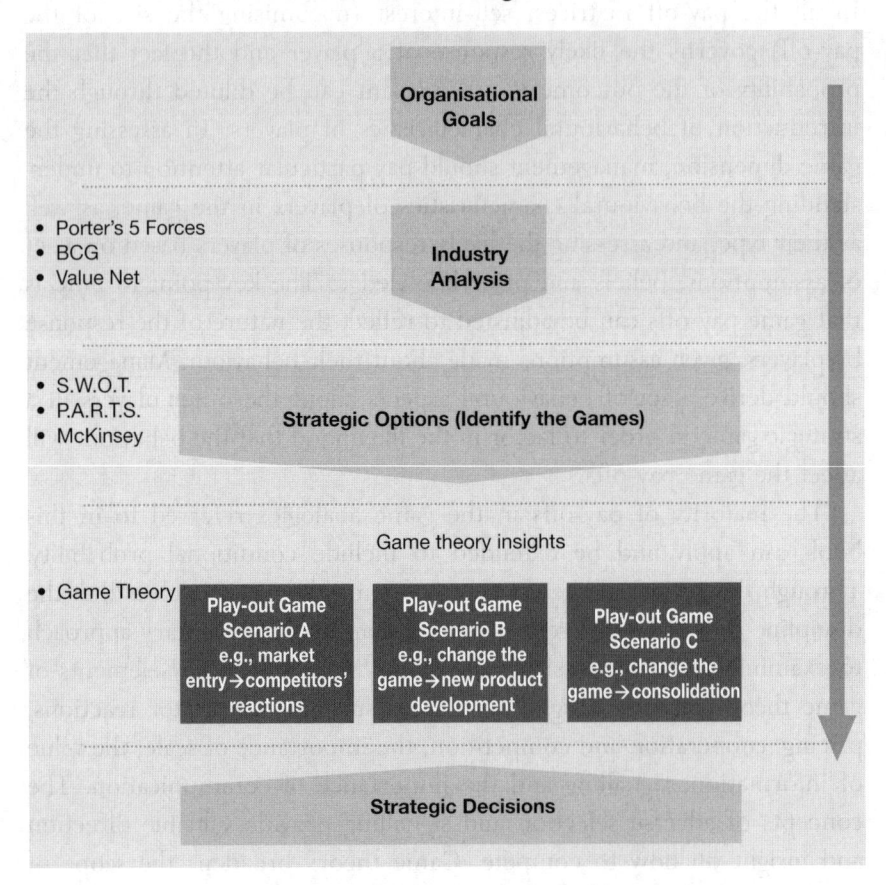

Organisational Goals

- Porter's 5 Forces
- BCG
- Value Net

Industry Analysis

- S.W.O.T.
- P.A.R.T.S.
- McKinsey

Strategic Options (Identify the Games)

Game theory insights

- Game Theory

| Play-out Game Scenario A e.g., market entry → competitors' reactions | Play-out Game Scenario B e.g., change the game → new product development | Play-out Game Scenario C e.g., change the game → consolidation |

Strategic Decisions

In Table 9.7, the win-win payoff (2,2) for both players is to play SA, and signal type.

Table 9.7
Prisoners' Dilemma

	SA	SB
SA: (Signal your type)	2,2	−1,3
SB: (Act differently)	3,−1	0,0

Samuelson (2005) reported that in laboratory experiments on PD games some players preferred the more superior outcome (2,2). In a business context, where the market is a game, and where type is either signalled by all players or analysed by third parties, the DQ player may prefer the more equal, although firm-specific, less profitable outcome of SA to the more asymmetric pay-offs obtained under SB. If both players adopt SA we observe a penguin strategy – a credible collective response by competitors to a market event such that no one competitor acts unilaterally and all competitors are observed to behave together. It can give rise to an accidental sameness in price (ASP) observation absent tacit collusion as argued in McNutt's *Law, Economics and Antitrust* (2005). This would be a defining characteristic of a game embedded strategy.

CHAPTER 10

Market Systems

> "Not one of them was capable of lying,
> There was not one which knew that it was dying
> Or could have a rhythm or a rhyme,
> Assumed responsibility for time."
>
> *W.H. Auden*

In the discussion of the market-as-a-game, we are proposing that competition is a process and that the game is necessary because of its function as a determination of evolving market systems. The process could be described as efficient contracting between firms. To put it another way, competition in an evolving market system can be viewed as an assignment of property rights to the market system rents (McNutt, 2005). Management should enquire whether the (p,q) pair is a strategic outcome, and whether it is stable in an evolving market system. In other words, will (p,q) persist, and if a firm chooses their actions from that pair, will the choice of price and quantity continue to distribute rents to the firm? In an evolutionary game setting, being able to choose may well turn out to be a disadvantage (Maynard Smith, 1982). This is tantamount to there being no choice for the firm.

Defining a Boolean Network of Competition

Game embedded strategy (GEMS) works on the assumption that there is a **Boolean network** of firm behaviour; the intuition is as follows: firm conduct in the assignment of market system rents is what it is because were it different, business activity as we know it would not exist and we would not be able to calculate the monopoly burdens or welfare measures. At its simplest, a Boolean network provides for a decision, which stipulates that each firm in a market with n firms acts (say, on price or on R&D expenditure or on innovation) if, and only if, two or more firms act. For example, firm A makes a decision if two other firms make a decision, but each firm can decide to act or not at each decision point.

While this can be generalised to explain the quintessence of aggressive competition, its central message is that for a random firm in an evolving market system its behaviour on price and quantity may be fixed exogenously. So, for example, a random firm offers n products and for each feasible bundle q it charges a price p(q). Profit is strictly a function of the prices. Each customer responds by choosing its preferred bundle and paying the price. The firm's objective in choosing the price is to maximise its profit contribution, obtained as the difference between the revenues collected and the costs it incurs to supply the bundles demanded. The firm incurs this cost only if a customer purchases a non-negative amount of some product. The prices evolve as marginal prices (Wilson, 1991), since they are observed as partial sums of the associated prices for incremental bundles of product.

Standard and Zero Sum

The standard economic model of collusion begins with the assumption that cartels are costless to form and maintain. But cartels accrue costs, for example the costs of monitoring cheats. Johnsen, in a classic article on the assignment of property rights to cartel rents, argued that "maximising cartel wealth translates into maximising the discounted value of the difference between gross cartel rents and cartel enforcement costs" (Johnsen, 1991, p. 189). The closer the cartel comes to the (p,q) that maximises gross cartel rents, the greater the incentive for members to cheat.

The key to applying the concept of tacit collusion is to distinguish tacit collusion from competitive aggressive behaviour. In any defence of an alleged price-fixing case, the mere fact of adherence to prices may not

Figure 10.1
ASP and Zero Sum

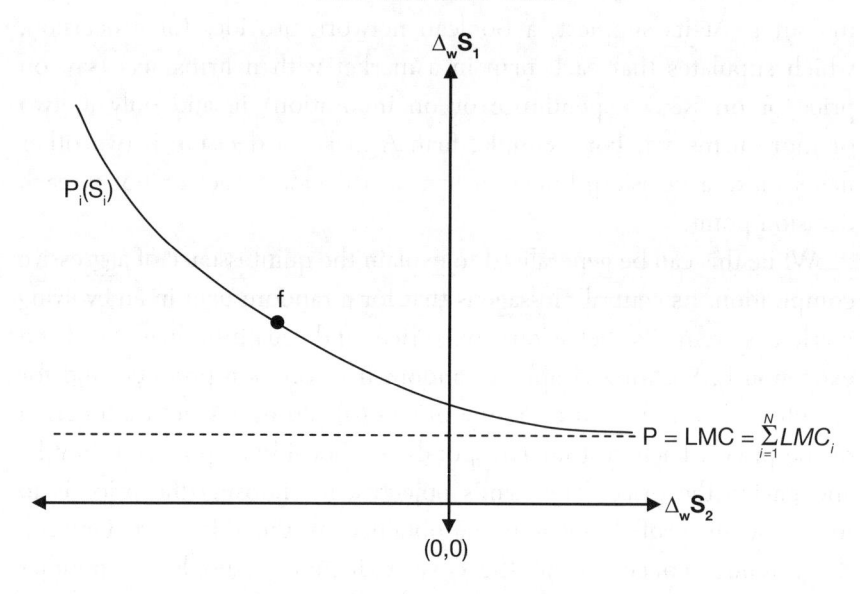

$$\Delta_w S_1$$ (vertical axis, up)
$$\Delta_w S_2$$ (horizontal axis, right)
$P_i(S_i)$
f
$P = LMC = \sum_{i=1}^{N} LMC_i$
$(0,0)$

establish an agreement to adhere to them (McNutt, 2003). Therefore, it would be unlikely for a competition court to find that adherence alone could prove, beyond all reasonable doubt, an agreement to adhere to prices; there may be 'an asymptote in prices' (ASP) observed as an accidental sameness in price across the market.

In Figure 10.1, market shares are denoted by s. Introduce a zero-sum assumption, which implies that as the market share of firm 1 (S_1) increases, the market share of firm 2 (S_2) decreases, as noted in the left-hand quadrant. This would represent a classic case of real competition characterised by competitive aggressive behaviour through loss in market share. The history of market price is represented by the function $P_i(S_i)$, which is asymptotic to a lower bound, $P = LMC$, the long-run competitive price for the market in which these two firms interact. The loss in market shares accruing to any one firm is represented by Δ_w.

The Boolean network provides for a competitive zero-sum rule, $\Delta_w x_i$, as follows:

$$\Delta_w x_i = x_i - w_i = \{(1, -1), i = 1 \ \& \ (-1, 1), i = 2\}$$

Markets can be either collusive or competitive. But firms in both situations behave rationally and independently. However, tacit collusion needs some form of an enforcement mechanism to sustain a coordinated equilibrium at f in Figure 10.1. In the absence of such a credible mechanism, the market price at f could be described as the price at a point in the history of the market moving towards a long-run competitive price. It is the market characteristics and the history of prices therein that make a market more collusive and less competitive. An ASP price standard is asymptotically close to a long-run competitive price. It therefore follows that not all instances of parallel behaviour could give rise to the same strength of inference that the parallelism results from anything other than the independent commercial judgement of the firms in a Boolean network.

Price Coordination

Economic theory would have us believe that price coordination is designed to reduce the uncertainty associated with interdependence and thereby decrease the likelihood of mutually destructive price competition. Consider n-player rent and profits games. The player set, the set of firms $\{1, 2, 3, \ldots n\}$, is denoted by N, the set of coalitions by 2^N. Such a game is a real valued function v: $2^N \rightarrow R$ with v(0), which assigns to each coalition, S, its worth v(S). The worth v(S) can be interpreted as the reward, which the players in S can obtain by working together. We denote the set of n-person rent and profits games by G_n. The main problem in cooperative game theory for analysts is how to divide v(N) among the players if the grand coalition forms.

There are many solutions, and they offer competition policy economists and lawyers a new tool of analysis and set of defences respectively: in some games, for example, the dividend of any one player is proportional to the marginal contributions of the players to the grand coalition (Owen, 1982). The marginal contributions are captured by movements along the $P_i(S_i)$ function in Figure 10.2. This is analogous to the biological concept of 'carrying capacity', that is, the maximum number of firms that can be sustained by a given amount of resources. It is not unlike an optimal club size in the provision of public goods (McNutt, 2002).

Later in this chapter, we include this as the parameter K in the equations for contest competition. Intuitively, one knows that not every firm can adapt to external threats, and with the passage of time only a few large firms will survive.

Perfect information amongst businesses would allow some to quickly enter the price-fixed markets and compete away the supra-competitive profits. The competition would soon drive prices down to only an insignificant fraction above the competitive level (Averitt and Lande, 1997). As the industrial (business) stage in different jurisdictions assumes the status of an oligopoly, there may be increasing support for the argument that a measure of price coordination is necessary in an oligopolistically structured industry. Innovation may require firms to enter complex contracts and relationships with other firms in order to bring technology to the economic market. But uncertainty is high. The uncertainty is especially high for the development and commercialisation of new technology. Accordingly, innovating firms may need to achieve greater coordination than the price system alone appears to be able to bring about (Jorde and Teece, 1990).

Scramble, Combat and Contest

Imagine that there are n operating firms in a market that is viable for only m < n. This may, for example, be the case in markets wherein technology or innovation involves a fixed cost of production. Selection may then operate in order for the firms not to lose money. Fudenberg and Tirole (1986) examine how the remaining firms are picked in order to explain why selection is not immediate, that is, why there are periods of time over which firms lose money but do not leave the market. They find it difficult to pin down a stable equilibrium outcome and conclude that there is a strictly positive but possibly small probability that the firm, as a player in a game, 'enjoys fighting'.

To put it another way, a firm with strictly positive duopoly profit never drops out of a market – staying in the market is a dominant strategy. Biologists have also analysed this type of situation. For example, animals may spend time or energy in a seemingly useless fight for prey (Maynard Smith, 1974). Firms may persist in a market. Therefore, firm 1, if it observes that firm 2 is still in at time t, ought to infer that firm 2 has a positive duopoly profit, and therefore will not drop out. Then firm 1, if it has a negative duopoly profit, ought to leave.

Moore's 'Form of Friction'

The fluctuation in the population of firms describes the process of competition. Much earlier in the history of economics, at a time when the Principles of Marshall were the subject of debate amongst Sraffa (1926) and Hotelling (1929), who laid the intellectual foundations for the concept of imperfection in the market, Moore (1906) offered a critical observation that has influenced the discussion in this chapter. Writing in the *Quarterly Journal of Economics*, Moore (1906) asked: "What is the nature of the limitation of the applicability of propositions under the hypothesis of perfect competition? The almost invariable answer to this question is that the imperfection of competition is simply *a form of friction*, producing for the most part, a negligible variation from the standards that prevail in a regime of perfect competition" (p. 211, italics added).

At the turn of the 20th century, the rigours of biology and physics were available to aspiring economists intent on developing an intellectual foundation for economics. Marshall opted for the rigours of physics in writing his *Principles* rather than the mathematical modelling of ecological systems. May (1973) commented that such models aim to provide a conceptual framework for the discussion of broad classes of phenomena. But Moore was asking a question, which could be answered only in the context of understanding the evolution of firms and markets. In trying to adapt what Moore may have meant by 'friction', we introduce types of competition adapted from models for species competition in biology (Hassell, 1976).

Types of Competition

One type of competition is **scramble competition**, wherein there is an exact equal partitioning of the market and hence an equal division of the effects of competition between the competitors. Scramble may be manifested by changes in the size of firms or number of firms. A second type of competition is **combat competition**, where the acquisition of market share requires constant defence. This would be characteristic of a more stable market system. Combat competition may be about entry at the margin and would manifest itself when an increasing number of firms is not an advantage to the market system. And finally, a third type of competition is **contest competition**, where the market is unequally partitioned in that some firms are content with their market shares while other firms are targets of merger or takeover.

Contest would occur, for example, where individual firms compete either for a given market share or for market position. Contest competition can be seen as a mechanism that tends to maintain the market level of concentration as long as the number of firms does not change. One essential characteristic of contest and scramble is that in both cases there is no exit of firms below a threshold level of concentration when there is ample market share for all competing firms. Above this threshold level of concentration, exit increases abruptly in the case of perfect scramble but gradually in the case of perfect contest. This follows necessarily from the requirement that contest leaves a constant number of firms in the market system.

It is conceivable that all competition under normal market conditions could fall between these idealised extremes of contest and scramble. Pure contest is rare; as individual firms compete for market share, there will often be a compromise as combat competition becomes more intense and average market share may be reduced. Larger firms will evolve and survive as they can provide economies of scale in production and innovation. Large firm size becomes essential to the success of innovative activity. With economies of scale, large firms make available sufficient resources for new innovative activity.

This process is not dissimilar to Schumpeter's cycle of 'creative destruction' in which old industrial structures, their products, their manufacturing processes and their organisational form are continually changed by new innovative activity. Schumpeter's (1934) original hypothesis was that economic growth occurs through a process of 'creative destruction' and that long-term growth is intricately linked with innovation. The introduction of a new good or new quality of an existing good, the introduction of a new method of technology, the introduction of a new organisational form or the opening of a new market are all characteristics of a market system.

In understanding how a market system differs from a market structure, we need to acknowledge that firms in a market structure cannot easily adapt internally to an external threat. The classic monopoly firm has little or no incentive to change if the status quo is profitable. Incumbents may attempt to retard entry. The classic monopoly and the incumbent both suffer from a 'box-ticking exercise' whereby behaviour and conduct is predetermined by the structure of the market. It is as if the very structure of the market creates what Nolan and Croson (1995) called 'structural inertia'. In contrast, firms evolve in a market system, making radical changes in both strategy and organisation in the face of external threats. The s-firm, for example, is an internal response from the workers and management to the external threat of unemployment.

Modelling Contest Competition

The specification of the entry function and its concavity in Chapter 6 highlighted the restrictive nature of entry. E(q) translated into an actual market share if entry was impeded. In a market system, all firms (potential entrants and incumbents) have the potential to grow exponentially, as expressed by the system equation,

$$dn/dt = r.n$$

Thus, the rate of change in the number of firms, n, with the passage of time, t, is the product of the numbers of firms and their intrinsic rate of natural increase, r. This is the maximum instantaneous rate of increase under the Scherer and Ross (1990) conditions for competition. To find the number of firms at any given time t, we integrate to get

$$n_t = n_0 e^{rt}$$

where n_0 is the number of firms at time t_0. From this, we can plot the exponential growth of the number of firms with time. However, no firms can sustain such an increase for long. Competition for resources will become increasingly more acute and the net rate of increase [dn/dt] reduced, either due to mergers or acquisitions, exit of firms or both. Therefore, the market system can be described as

$$dn/dt = r.n \{(\beta - n)/\beta\}$$

where β is the 'carrying capacity' of the system at a point in time – the maximum number of firms that can be sustained by a given amount of limited resources. If we use the firms' production levels at $t \geq 0$ as a proxy for the amount of limited resources, the carrying capacity could be defined as

$$CC = (\text{firm's production levels})^{-n}/\{n/n + 1\}^n$$

The emphasis is on the available carrying capacity at $t \geq 0$. Knowledge of rising scale economies may not be known to the fact finder at $t = t_0$. The number of firms may fall as firms merge to gain efficiencies. The available carrying capacity is an important part of the determination of whether a merger may lead to a dominant position or whether a given market share level may converge towards a collusive outcome. Using integration, we have

$$n_t = \beta/\{1 + q.e^{-rt}\}$$

where $q = \beta/2$ is the point of inflexion on the time axis as illustrated in Figure 10.2, adapted from Varley (1973). The growth in the number of firms can be described as sigmoid. It commences almost exponentially, but as the number of firms increases there is more and more feedback from the term $[(\beta - n)/\beta]$, representing the effects of increased competition. A rapidly growing firm in contest competition may be more likely to make a horizontal acquisition because it would be better able to use the additional capacity. The net rate of increase thereof declines until, when the carrying capacity is reached, $[n_t = \beta]$, there is no further change in the number of firms. And the market system is therefore at equilibrium, $[n^* = \beta]$.

The model offers a stable equilibrium since the number of firms will always return to its equilibrium following an external threat or

**Figure 10.2
Contest Competition**

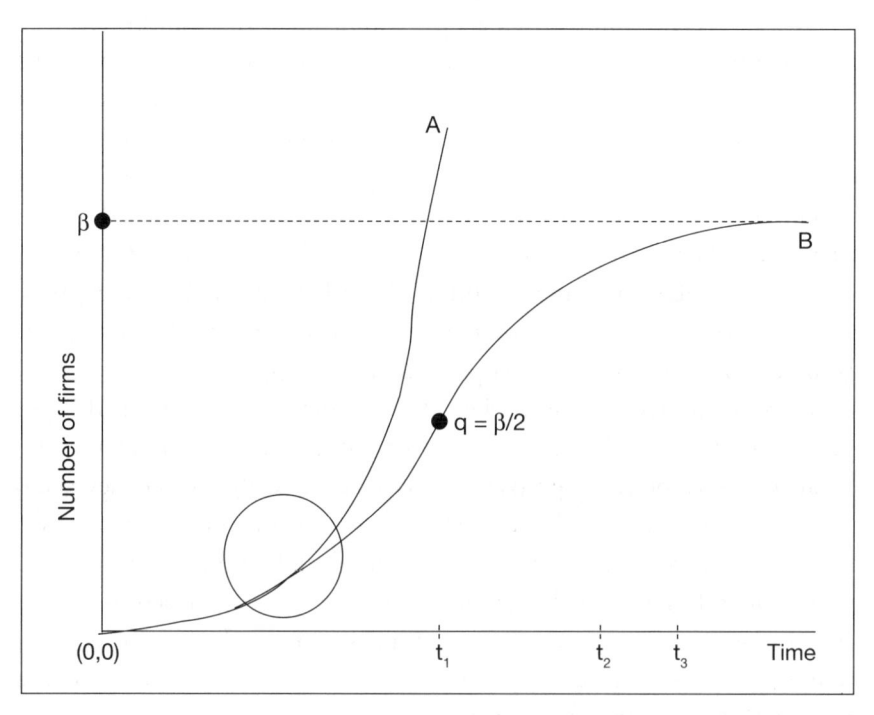

[Figure: Graph with "Number of firms" on y-axis and "Time" on x-axis. Point β marked on y-axis with dashed horizontal line to point B. Curve A rises steeply; another curve passes through point q = β/2 and asymptotes to B. A circle highlights the region near the origin where curves intersect. Time markers t_1, t_2, t_3 on x-axis, origin at (0,0).]

disturbance. For example, a declining firm operating under diseconomies of scale will be more likely to sell and exit the system. Tremblay (1987) found that a firm with large economies of scale will have a greater incentive to merge if the economies are multi-plant in nature. The essential economic character of what is observed at $t \geq 0$ is one of contest competition; the maximum number of firms is independent of the initial density of firms.

Spherical Competitors

The basic conditions of the market system, the carrying capacity, can plausibly explain the evolution of the system. The litmus test is whether the fact finder can define the market within an evolutionary system. Much depends on what the fact finder observes at the critical juncture in the evolution of the system, as illustrated by the circle in Figure 10.2. The point of departure within the circle can be changed by the internal dynamics of each firm in the system. Path A is the exponential evolutionary path, which may not be sustainable – it represents intense aggressive competition, with entry and exit of firms. It may, for example, characterise atomistic perfect competition in classical economics. However, once the surviving firms have established a level of market share, path B can better describe the evolution of a system more closely aligned to the evolution of markets in classical economics, from a starting position of competitive market, through the emergence of monopoly firms and an oligopoly structure capped at β.

In concentrated markets, where five or fewer players share 100 per cent market share, the zero-sum constraint allows each player to infer what the other player is prepared to sacrifice, and thus what they stand to gain by an action. Without knowing how much market share a player has, for example, a rival cannot really know whether an action on price is meaningful or not. If the action on price can be described as a price dwarf, and if a rival is to react at time period t, then knowledge of market share is invaluable, because in its absence a reaction to such a price action could trigger a price war.

Technology has a long history that dates back many centuries. From the ox cart to the car, from the mainframe to the laptop, technology gaps are diminishing and consumer expectations are increasing. Many players are moving under the influence of each other's technology pull. Some are moving unexpectedly fast as though being pulled by an invisible time-dependent set of preferences. The β is defining the process of competition. The competitors are spherical competitors, since the technology allows competition from every angle. Observations of the signals, together with managerial theories about how management behave and have evolved, all point to Framework $Tn=3$. But the theory of firm behaviour combined with observations would suggest that β is too lightweight to account for all competition that $\beta = n. [dT.dt]$ in that one can observe β but cannot define it.

Figure 10.3 captures a stylised game pay-off between player A and player B on the level of price commitment. The pay-offs are computed

Figure 10.3
Hsu-McNutt Signalling

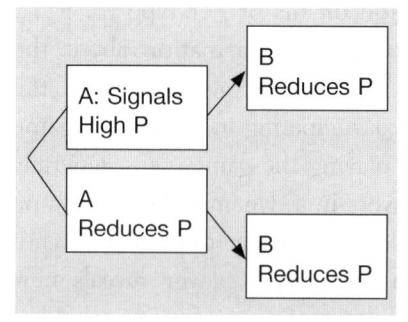

	B Signals High Price	B Reduces Price
A Signals High Price	(4,3)	(3,4)
A Reduces Price	(5,1)	(1,1)

Decision tree:
- A: Signals High P → B Reduces P
- A Reduces P → B Reduces P

by McNutt and Yang-Chan Hsu as illustrative of existing Nash equilibria in terms of the best one can do given the reaction of a competitor and the elusive (4,3) that could be secured with price leadership – provided both players trust each other not to deviate from the agreed price leadership. The game dimension in terms of near rival may differ according to geography. For example, Nissan and Toyota are near rivals in Japan, but it is possible that in Europe the players could be Nissan and Volkswagen. Notwithstanding geography and type, an equilibrium requires a degree of trust and commitment to be signalled.

Critical Reflective Thinking

In this book, we have argued that type is a function of signals; in other words, a signal is the first derivative of type with respect to time. At a point in time $t = T$, individual players learn from each other through signalling. No action is observed from a player until the player filters the information from the signal. In the case of a moon-shot (see Chapter 1), a player believes that the signal will translate into an action, thus he proceeds to act and is observed by other players. With signalling, a player stops and thinks; no action is observed at $t = T$, referred to as a do-nothing strategy. This differs from the mechanism of observational learning, where the action of one player is influenced by their observation of other players' actions. McNutt (2005) commented that

"Bayesian equilibrium does not take into account the fact that players may learn their opponents' **types** by observing their play, since each move by a player may reveal information on his or her type (p. 92)". In a Bayesian game, players have incomplete information about the characteristics of the other players. Management as players in the market-as-a-game can be described as participating in a Bayesian game and the signals on type are critical to playing the game. It is generally agreed amongst game theorists that players in a dynamic Bayesian game of incomplete information, players do learn their opponents' types by observing their play, because each move by a player reveals new information on a player's type. In the absence of new information, there is a challenge for a Bayesian market-as-a-game if others do not know, for example, that Player A in Figure 10.3 has betrayed his type — deceiving other players by signalling a high price but reducing price during the game. The Bayesian updating by other players relies on the observed action of Player A without reference to the formation or origin of the beliefs about Player A. Competitors should ask: why would a rival player be observed as doing nothing in a game? In a normal form Bayesian game of incomplete information, the players are unable to update their prior beliefs on opponents' types. One way to model incomplete information is to reduce the uncertainty in the game and convert it into a game of imperfect information. In this case, all Player A knows is his own type, and the fact that the other players do not know his type.

Neo-Rational Action

Learning from others in the market-as-a-game requires the players to understand what we refer to as the Humean neo-rational action of a player, McNutt (2010) — that is, a player betrays his type during a game by signalling X but doing Y. In other words, if management want to do Y (reduce price) and believe that doing X (signal a high price) is causally necessary to do Y then reason directs that they signal X in the game. If Player A does play Y and lowers the price, and this action is consistent to include observations by others of the action of playing Y, then playing Y is a neo-rational action by Player A: he may obtain a payoff of 5. In other words, Player A has fooled others into thinking that he is thinking about playing X prior to his decision to do so. He has created noise in the game by signalling X but doing Y – possibly to obtain a payoff of 5 or he may do nothing. The market-as-a-game may be a Bayesian game in the sense that information about the economic characteristics and type of other individuals in the game is incomplete but beliefs only role with respect to the observed action and conduct of Player A is to achieve a coherence with Player B's intentions and the beliefs and preferences of other competitors about Player A. In the next section, the neo-rational equilibrium could occur at payoff (4,3) for both players in Figure 10.3 if Player A is secure and Player B is thinking that Player A is thinking about playing X.

Blind Squirrels Find Nuts

Bayesian equilibrium only takes into account the fact that players may learn their opponents' **actions** by observing their play. The Bayesian approach ignores a do-nothing strategy and it does not suggest a model on the origin of prior beliefs. In Framework $Tn=3$, beliefs are updated in the absence of new information. This arises because management have to focus on the origin of their respective belief about a competitor's likely action. Management as players in the market-as-a-game observe their opponents' types by observing their play but if no play or action is observed then management will learn-by-signalling. Hence, individual players are acting rationally at $t = T$ when they do not ignore their own information about signals but do ignore the actions of others.

In Framework $Tn=3$, a signal can influence the action of a player in a game. For example, in Figure 10.3, if at $t = K < T$, player B signals a Baumol type by signalling sales revenue targets, this very strongly implies that player B's prices will fall, but observing lower prices in a game at $t = T$ does not necessarily mean that player B is a Baumol type. For example, if a new technology or functionality was added to player B's product at $t = K$, creating an inelastic demand for the product, player B will increase price to maximise total revenues. Therefore, if the probability of lower prices in the absence of a Baumol type is greater than zero, the probability of lower prices with a Baumol type is less than one since the probabilities sum to one.

On the other hand, if lower prices did not happen when Player B was not a Baumol type, then observing that prices are lower at t = T in a game with Player B would always confirm that Player B is a Baumol type. Strategic reasoning is not the product of a very high probability that Y leads to X; that lower prices signal a Baumol type, but the product of a very **low** probability that **not-Y** (~Y) could have led to X. An error in the game occurs when too much attention is paid to p(X|Y) and not enough to p(X|~Y) when determining how much evidence X is for Y. The degree to which a result X is evidence for Y depends, not only on the strength of the statement 'we would expect to observe signal X if Y were true', but also on the strength of the statement 'we would not expect to observe signal X if Y were not true'. If Player B in Figure 10.3 is a Baumol type and always reduces price then it is rational for Player B to signal type and to obtain the payoff 4 in (3,4) provided Player A does not lower price. With that knowledge, Player A as a secure player (Chapter 7) signals a high price trusting B to do likewise. For Player B, a 3 in payoff (4,3) is preferred to a payoff of 1 in (1,1).

Strategy is about independent action and reaction; it is a rule telling management which action to choose at any given time. Game embedded strategy is about knowing when and knowing how to act. Interdependence is recognised, beliefs are formed and management rethink the strategy of 'going it alone' in order to obtain a competitive advantage in the market.

Heraclitus, a Greek philosopher of the sixth century BC, wrote, "Character is destiny"; Framework $Tn=3$ recognises that management type is destiny, and that understanding type, coupled with understanding technology and time, is intricately linked to sustaining a competitive advantage in the market-as-a-game.

Bibliography

Averitt, N. and R. Lande (1997). "Consumer Sovereignty: A Unified Theory of Antitrust and Consumer Protection Law", *Antitrust Law Journal*, Vol. 65, No. 3, pp. 713–756.

Bartley, J. and C. Boardman (1986). "The Replacement-Cost-Adjusted Valuation Ratio as Discriminator Among Takeover Targets", *Journal of Economics and Business*, Vol. 2, pp. 41–55.

Baumol, W. (1967). "Calculation of Optimal Product and Retailer Characteristics", *Journal of Political Economy*, Vol. 25, pp. 187–198.

Baye, M. (2008). *Managerial Economics and Business Strategy*. New York: McGraw-Hill.

Berle, A.A. and G. Means (1932). *The Modern Corporation and Private Property*. New York: Macmillian.

Besanko, D., et al (2008). *Economics of Strategy*. USA: John Wiley & Sons.

Binmore, K. and P. Dasgupta (1986). *The Economics of Bargaining*. Oxford: Blackwell Publishers.

Chamberlin, E.H. (1962). *The Theory of Monopolistic Competition*. USA: Harvard University Press.

Chandler, A.D. (1962). *Strategy and Structure*. USA: Cambridge University Press.

Crawford, V. and N. Iriberri (2007). "Fatal Attraction Salience, Naivete and Sophistication in Experimental Hide-and-Seek Games", *American Economic Review*, Vol. 97 (December 2007), pp. 1731–1750.

Cubbin, J.S. (1988). *Market Structure and Performance*. NY: Harwood Academic Publishers.

Cyert, R. and J. March (1963). *Behavioural Theory of the Firm*. USA: Englewood Cliffs, NJ.

Davies, H. and P-L Lam (2001). *Managerial Economics*. UK: Prentice Hall.

Demsetz, H. (1973). "Industry Structure, Market Rivalry and Public Policy", *Journal of Law and Economics*, Vol. 16, No. 1, pp. 1–10.

Edgeworth, F.Y. (1881). *Mathematical Psychics*. USA: Kessinger Publications.

Ellsberg, D. (1961). "Risk, Ambiguity, and the Savage Axioms", *Quarterly Journal of Economics*, Vol. 75, No. 4, pp. 643–669.

Follett, M. (1924). *Creative Experience*. New York: Longman Green.

Friedman, J. (2000). "A Guided Tour of the Folk Theorem", in G. Norman and J-F Thisse [eds], *Market Structure and Competition Policy*. UK: Cambridge University Press.

Friedman, J., Jeheil, P. and J-F Thisse (1995). "Collusion and Antitrust Detection", *Japanese Economic Review*, Vol. 46, pp. 226–246.

Fudenberg, D. and J. Tirole (1986). *Dynamic Models of Oligopoly*. New York: Harwood Academic Publishers.

Gul, F. and W. Pesendorfer (2007). "Welfare Without Happiness", *American Economic Review*, May 2007, Vol. 97, No. 2, pp. 471–476.

Hagstrom, R. (2005). *The Warren Buffet Way*. US: John Wiley & Sons.

Hassell, M. (1976). "The Dynamics of Competition and Predation", *Studies in Biology*, No. 77. UK: Edward Arnold Publishers.

Hay, D. and D. Morris (1991). *Industrial Economics and Organisation*. Oxford: Oxford University Press.

Henrich, J. (2004). "Cultural Group Selection", *Journal of Economic Behaviour and Organisation*, Vol. 53, No. 1, pp. 3–35.

Hotelling, H. (1929). "Stability in Competition", *Economic Journal*, Vol. 39, No. 153, pp. 41–57.

Johnsen, D.B. (1991). "Property Rights to Cartel Rents", *Journal of Law and Economics*, Vol. 34, pp. 177–203.

Jones, T. (2004). *Business Economics and Management Decisions*. UK: John Wiley & Sons.

Jorde, T. and D. Teece (1990). "Innovation and Cooperation", *Journal of Economic Perspectives*, Vol. 4, No. 3, pp. 75–96.

Landes, W. and R. Posner (1981). "Market Power and Antitrust Cases", *Harvard Law Review*, Vol. 94, No. 5, pp. 937–996.

Leibenstein, H. (1976). *Beyond Economic Man*. USA: Harvard University Press.

Mahoney, J.T. (2005). *Economic Foundations of Strategy*. UK: Sage Publications.

Marris, R. (1966). *The Economic Theory of Managerial Capitalism* (2nd edition). UK: Macmillan.

May, R.M. (1973). *Stability and Complexity in Model Ecosystems*. USA: Princeton University Press.
Maynard-Smith, J. (1974). "The Theory of Games and the Evolution of Animal Conflict", *Journal of Theoretical Biology*, Vol. 47, pp. 209–221.
Maynard-Smith, J. (1982). *Evolution and the Theory of Games*. UK: Cambridge University Press.
McNutt, P. (2002). *Economics of Public Choice* (2nd edition). UK: Edward Elgar Publishing.
McNutt, P. (2003). "Taxonomy of Non-Market Economics for European Competition Policy", *World Competition*, Vol. 26, No. 2, pp. 303–332.
McNutt, P. (2005): *Law, Economics and Antitrust*. UK: Edward Elgar Publishing.
McNutt, P. (2008). *Signalling, Strategy and Management Type*. Ebook, available on www.patrickmcnutt.com.
McNutt, P. (2009). "Secrets and Lies: The Neighbourhood of No-Truth", *Homo Oeconomicus*, Vol. 26, No.1, pp. 161–171.
McNutt, P. (2010). *Political Economy of Law*. UK: Edward Elgar Publishing.
Moore, P.G. and H. Thomas (1976). *The Anatomy of Decisions*. UK: Penguin Books.
Mueller, D.C. (1972). "A Life Cycle Theory of the Firm", Journal of Industrial Economics, Vol. 20, No. 3, pp. 199–219.
Mun, T. (1664). *England's Treasure by Forraign Trade*. UK: Drury Rare Books.
Nalebuff, B. and A. Dixit (2008). *The Art of Strategy*. USA: W.W. Norton & Company.
Nolan, R.L. and D.C. Croson (1995). *Creative Destruction*. USA: Harvard University Press.
Owen, G. (1982). *Game Theory*. NY: Academic Press.
Reny P.J. (1993). "Common Belief and the Theory of Games with Perfect Information", *Journal of Economic Theory*, Vol. 59, No. 2, pp. 257–274.
Samuelson, L. (2005). "Foundations of Human Sociality: A Review Essay", *Journal of Economic Literature*, June 2005, Vol. 43, No. 2, pp. 488–497.
Schelling, T. (1960). *The Strategy of Conflict*. USA: Harvard University Press.
Scherer, F.M. and D. Ross (1990). *Industrial Market Structure and Economic Performance*. Chicago: Rand McNally.
Schumpeter, J. (1934). *The Theory of Economic Development*. US: Harvard University Press.
Shubik, M. (1960). *The Meaning of Modern Business*. NY: Columbia University Press.

Simon, H.A. (1958). *Organisations* [in collaboration with J. March and H. Guetzkow]. New York: John Wiley & Sons.
Sraffa, P. (1926). "Sulla Relazione Fra Costo e Quanta Prodotta", *Economic Journal*, Vol. December, pp. 277–378.
Tremblay, V. (1987). "Scale Economies Technological Change and Firm Cost Asymmetries in US Brewing", *Quarterly Review of Economics and Business*, Vol. 27, p. 71–86.
Varley, G.C. (1973). *Insect Population Ecology*. Oxford: Blackwell.
Von Neumann, J. and O. Morgenstern (1944). *Theory of Games and Economic Behaviour*. USA: Princeton University Press.
Vives, X. (2005). "Complementarities and Games: New Developments", *Journal of Economic Literature*, June 2005, Vol. 43, No. 2, pp. 437–479.
Wilson, R. (1991). "Multi-product Tariffs", *Journal of Regulatory Economics*, Vol. 3, pp. 5–26.

Index

Action-reaction-reply strategy, 66–67
Advertising elasticity of demand, *see* Price elasticity
Agency costs, 46–47
Alternative decision logic, 7
Ambush strategy, 27
Asymmetric sameness in price condition, 117–118
Average revenue per user, *see* 'Bums on seats' pricing

Back-scatter approach, 63
Backward induction, 95, 114
Bain-Modigliani model, *see* Limit pricing model
Balanced growth path (BGP), 38, 39, 43–44
Bargaining mechanism, 118
Baumol hypothesis, 9, 28–37
    Baumol type strategy, 31–32
    elasticity, 30–31
    elasticity and want paradox, 36–37
    market share gain, 34
    oligopoly, 29–30
    penetration pricing, 34
    price discrimination, 34–35
    sales fuel profits, 33–34
    tumbling price paradox, 32–33
Baumol type, 31–32, 84, 92, 93, 111
Bayesian game, 47, 146, 147
    Bayesian-type management, 97
    Bayesian-type rule, 15, 47
Behavioural approach, 15–17
Believable Bill type, 71–72
Bertrand dilemma, 123–124
Bertrand model, 112–113
Beyond Economic Man, 8
Blended management, 88
Boolean behaviour, 125
Boolean network of competition, 134–135, 136–137
Bounded rationality, 54, 109, 110
Boxticking exercise and market system, 141
'Bums on seats' pricing, 31

Capacite excedentaire, 58–59
Carrying capacity, 137, 142
Cartels, 24, 74, 87, 101, 104, 105, 117, 118, 123, 124–125, 135
Cash flow, 48, 50
Chamberlin model, 125
Chandler's thesis, 127
Collective bargaining, 8

Combat competition, 99, 100, 106, 123, 124, 125, 138, 140
Conjectural variation, 79, 81, 82, 111, 119
Contest competition, 99, 100, 106, 110, 123–124, 125, 138, 140, 141–143
Cooperative pricing, 116
Cost leadership, 54, 55, 60, 62
  five-step analysis, 61
Cost technology, 53–63
  cost leadership type, 60, 62
  excess versus reserve capacity, 58–60
  production-demand dilemma, 55–56
  wage normalisation, 56–57
Cournot-Nash play, 117, 126
Creative destruction, 140
Creative Experience, 8
Critical reflective thinking, 145–146
Critical timeline (CTL), 6, 19–20, 27, 91
  Apple v Nokia, 92, 93
  Apple v RIM, 93, 94
  Nissan, 20
  Sony v Microsoft, 115

Dark strategy, 77–97
  belief system, 79–80
  burden of loss standard, 86–87
  dark strategy mistakes, 95
  decision quantum, 81–84
  mistake-proofing, 78–79
  noise, 91–92
  poka-yoke, 84–86, 88
  strategic behaviour, 80–81
  strategy set, 87–89
  Z or third variable, 89–91
Decision quantum, 81–84, 106, 110
Demand elasticity, 112
Demand for capital (gd) equation, 41–42, 44, 45
De Nihilo Nihil Fit, 63
De novo type player, 71, 72, 73, 74, 75
Diversification acreage, 47–48
Dividends paradox, 42
Dividends versus R&D trade-off, 40
Dominant strategy, 69–70
Doubting Thomas type, 72–73

Easterbrook–McNutt strategic tool-box GEMS, 132
Economies of scale, 61–62
Edgeworth constraint, 3
Efficient entry price, 99
Endogenous rival type, 74–75
Error, 118–119
Excess capacity, 55, 56, 58–60, 76, 117
Extant type players, 73, 82, 83

Financial elasticity measure, 46
Folk theorem, 104, 116
Framework $Tn=3$, 1, 2, 3, 5, 6, 7, 8, 10, 11, 14, 16, 19, 29, 38, 39, 42, 46, 49, 55, 66, 78, 89, 91, 95, 107, 119, 127, 128, 129, 144, 147, 148
Functionalities, 60

Game Embedded Strategy (GEMS), 18–27, 129, 131–133, 134
  ambush strategy, 27
  characteristics, 127

critical timeline, 19–20
dimensions, 129
market type, 25–26
Nash premise, 23–24
Penrose effect, 22–23
strategy toolbox, 131–133
zero-sum constraint, 21
Game theory, 2, 3, 4, 5, 9, 15, 24, 26, 66, 67, 79, 82, 96, 99, 104, 111
Ghost demand, 63

Homo ludens (game-playing man), 98, 99
  decision quantum, 106
  first hurdle initiative, 102–103
  market systems, 99–101, 106–108
  mixed strategy, 105–106
  Nash equilibrium, 101–102
  Prisoner's dilemma, 103–104
SMIN©, 106–107
Hsu-McNutt signalling, 145

Incumbent type player, 71, 74, 82
Indifference analysis, 10–11
Interdependence, 21, 25

Jungle Warfare, 27

Kaizen, 84
Koeller-Lechler equation, 41

Law, Economics and Antitrust, 101, 102, 133
Limit pricing model, 67–68, 76
Long-run operating equilibrium, 45
Low-cost airlines (LCA) pricing model, 36

Management and decision-making, 81
Management team interaction, 83
Management type, 2, 5, 8–10, 12–13, 16, 19, 21, 24, 25, 26, 29, 35, 38, 46, 49, 51, 64, 67, 81, 82, 84, 86, 87, 106, 148
Management utility, 89–90
Market-as-a-game, 9–10, 108–133
  asymmetric sameness in price condition, 117–118
  Bertrand dilemma and trust, 123–124
  Bertrand model, 112–113
  error in game, 118–119
  folk theorem benefit-cost condition, 116
  game assumption, 109
  GEMS, 129, 131–133, 134
  homo ludens, 110–112
  market nature, to enter, 127–130
  Nash equilibrium, 114–116
  player assumption, 108
  price tumbles, 112
  regret matrix, 119–121
  saddle point market shares, 121–123
  Stigler's dilemma, 124–126
  symmetry, 110
  trigger price, 126
Market elasticity of demand, 116
Market systems, 99–101, 134–148
  Boolean network of competition, 134–135
  competition types, 139–141
  contest competition, modelling, 141–143
  critical reflective thinking, 145–146

Moore's form of friction, 139
price coordination, 137–138
spherical competitors, 143–145
standard and zero-sum, 135–137
Marris hypothesis, 9, 38–52
agency costs, 46–47
balanced growth path, 42–43
demand for capital (gd) equation, 41–42
dividends paradox, 42–43
dividends versus R&D trade-off, 40
Marris signalling, 51–52
Marris type positive learning transfer, 48–51
Marris v, 46
quasi-Marris model, 44–46
Maximal differentiation principle, 34
Maximax strategy, 120
Maximin strategy, 120
Minimax strategy, 122
Minimum efficient scale of operation, 58
Mistake-proofing, 63; *see also* Poka-yoke
Mixed strategy, 105–106
Model-T effect, 21
Moon-shot, 77–78, 96, 123
Mun's strategy, 34

Nash equilibrium, 101–103
realisation, 114–116
Nash premise, 5, 21, 23–25, 80, 90
Near-rival competitor, 95–97
Nearest rival, 3, 128
Neoclassical profit maximization models, 7
Neo-rational action, 146–147
Newborn player, 71
Noise, 91–92, 96, 147
in tumbling price, 92–94
Non-cooperation with mutual interdependence, 26
Non-cooperative game theory, 9, 67, 81, 123

Occam's razor, 109
Oligopoly, 9, 21, 24, 29–30, 66, 82, 86, 109, 112–113, 125, 129, 138, 144
One-shot price, 111
Organic growth, 9
Ovi, 91

Parallel behaviour, conscious, 124
Patterns and critical timeline, 20
Pay-off, 15, 23, 24, 70, 90, 100, 101, 104, 105, 106, 111, 119, 120, 121, 131, 133, 144
Penetration pricing, 34
Penrose effect, 22–23, 78, 79, 80, 81
Pessimism criterion, 120
Player type, 64, 67
Player types and signals, 71
Poka-yoke, 84–86, 88; *see also* Mistake-proofing
Porter's 5 Forces strategy, 128
Positive learning transfer (PLT), 13–15, 43, 46, 49
Marris type, 47–48
Potential entrant type player, 71, 72, 74
Premium, on type, 12–13

Price coordination, 137–138
Price discrimination, 34–35
Price dwarf, 144
Price elasticity, 28, 30–31, 35, 36, 37, 126
Price follower type, 9, 10
Price war, 10, 33, 67, 73–74, 81, 85, 98, 112, 113, 114, 116, 118, 123, 124, 126, 144
Principles of Marshall, 139
Prisoners' Dilemma (PD), 23, 100, 103–104, 105, 133
 social preference and, 107
Production-demand dilemma, 54, 55–56
Production relationship, 55
Production smoothing, 53
Punishment strategy, 101

Quarterly Journal of Economics, 139
Quasi-Marris model, 44–45

Rank and type, 73
Reciprocal price, 112
Regret matrix, 119–121
Reply strategy, 83
Reserve capacity, 54, 55, 58–60
Retaliation, 68–69
Risk-averse management, 84, 89

Saddle point market shares, 121–123
Sales fuel profits, 33–34
Satisficing, 7
Scramble competition, 99, 100, 106, 138, 139–140
Second-mover advantage, 78, 129
Secure player, 148
Security parameter, Marris, 52

Sherman Act (US), 124
Short-run cost curve, theoretical, 58
Signalling, 65, 73, 117
 business strategy, 5
 Marris type, 51–52
SMIN$^{©}$, 106–107
Spherical competitors, 143–145
Stigler's dilemma, 124–126
Strategic focus, Dell's movement in, 127
Strategic pricing, 112
Strategic reasoning, 1–18
Strategy equation, 80–81
Strategy set, 6, 24, 69, 86, 87–89, 121
Structural inertia, 141
Sun Tzu, 99
Supply correspondence dilemma, 78
Supply elasticity, 116
Switching costs, 32

Tacit collusion, 117, 133, 135, 137
Third variable, *see* Z variable
Trade-off, 7, 9, 10–11, 12, 13, 14, 17, 40, 41, 42, 43, 45, 49, 51, 80, 89
Trigger price, 126, *see also* Tumbling price paradox
Trust and Bertrand dilemma, 123–124
Tumbling price paradox, 4, 32–33

Uncertainty, 7, 18, 67, 95, 107, 108, 137, 138, 146

Vertical blending, 64–76, 129–130
 action-reaction-reply strategy, 66–67

believable Bills type, 72
dominant strategy, 69–70
'doubting Thomas' type, 72–73
signalling, 65
entry function and technology, 75–76
limit pricing model, 67–68
player types and signals, 71–72
rank and type, 73–75
retaliation, 68–69
signalling, 65, 73
Volunteer's Dilemma, 102–103
Von Neumann, 109
v variable, Marris, 46

Wage normalisation, 56–57
Want paradox, 37

Yield per passenger, *see* 'Bums on seats' pricing

Z variable, 10, 11, 13, 14, 30, 44, 45, 49, 50, 51, 89–91
Zero-price solution (Betrand solution), 113
Zero sum, 135–137
  constraint, 2, 3, 21–22, 24, 30, 39, 55, 66, 77, 80, 87, 112, 144
  game, 3, 98, 110, 122
  game theory, 24
  market, 80
  rule, 136–137